Stories From My Life

Rev. Fred H. Oldnall

Clink
Street

London | New York

Published by Clink Street Publishing 2015

Copyright © 2015

First edition.

ISBN: 978-1-910782-41-5
E-Book: 978-1-910782-42-2

Preface

This book is not the story of my life, in the biographical sense; instead I wish to simply share my experiences and feelings with others with the hope that their lives may be somewhat enriched by my words. It is written entirely from memory.

Much of my success in life I owe to my wife and certainly others of whom you will read.

I owe thanks to my daughter, without whom this book would not have been written.

Chapter 1

The school had been built in 1812. The building was red brick with a slate roof and was rather squat; it was situated between a high church wall and the busy main road. It was a Church of England school and placed near the parish church. The interior was dominated by three huge fireplaces, which in winter were piled high with coals. A large folding screen was used to divide the building into two rooms. There were two playgrounds: one on one side, and another the other side. The smaller one on the north side had a fenced off portion which was a shrubbery.

This, a decade before, had been the village pound. The pound keeper, Isaac George, had walked from Upton on Severn in search of work. When he reached Handsworth he was given a cottage and the job of pound keeper for five pounds a year. He afterwards became the village blacksmith and learnt to ring the church bells.

Pupils were taken up to the age of seven, when

they were transferred to a senior school. On my fifth birthday or thereabouts, in 1921, my mother took me to the school. I was taken to this school because my father and other children in his family had been pupils there in days gone by. I remember being taken into a large room where behind an enormous table sat a plump middle-aged lady known as Miss Andrews, who after a few words with my mother led me into an adjoining room. I was made to sit at a small desk with other children. A Miss Jones, a tall thin maiden lady, was in charge. I was told I was in the babies' class, and was given a slate and slate pencil and left there to draw with that very elementary equipment.

I remember the next day these were removed and I was given a sheet of paper and a pencil. Next, I remember some days later the head mistress Miss Andrews stood at the entrance to the room and shouted in a loud voice, "Form up, all those going to church." Ten or so children in pairs held hands and formed a queue. I do not know why but for some quite unknown reason I left my seat and joined at the end of the queue.

It was a mixed school so I probably held the hand of a little girl. Then I remember being marched in the morning sunlight down the road to the church. Unusually on this occasion the entrance to the church was by a small side door. Inside was a steep step down into semi darkness. The Head Mistress stood inside the door to ensure the careful entrance of each child. I arrived the last in the queue.

I shall never forget to this day the look of astonishment on her face when she saw me; her large eyes seemed to bulge with a stare, and in a loud voice she cried, "What on earth are you doing here?" I felt petrified and remember it to this day. Unusually small due to under nourishment, feeling weak and frightened, I could not speak. She must have seen before her a small and frightened, child; these were the days that children "should be seen and not heard".

All seemed still for a short time, then suddenly her whole face softened and she said, in a soft gentle voice, "Well, you are here and had better come in." She clasped my hand; thus did the hand of a good lady lead a small frightened child of God into the church of God.

Miss Andrews was a fine Christian woman and she taught us how to pray. At four o'clock (going home time), she called us all together for prayers. "Stand perfectly still, hands together, eyes closed." We learnt the Lord's Prayer line by line, repeating after her. Then she said the beautiful prayer, "Lighten our darkness we beseech thee oh Lord," … finally the words of the Grace. The busy main road lay outside the school, so she saw every child across the road safely.

When I was six years old, I went to the family Christmas party at my Granny's (my mother's mother) and her son-in-law, my Uncle Len. After tea he produced a crystal set and with much trouble tuned it into a London wireless station. He then announced the Archbishop of

Canterbury – the first broadcast of its nature. Everyone had a chance to listen with the earphones. I listened for half a minute. The voice was faint and faraway but I could make out a word or two. Afterwards I was asked to recite, "Do No Sinful Action," but later I had to recite the dreadful poem about a small boy's guilt, "Who Stole the Bird's Nest".

Some six months later, when I was seven, my Grandmother took me to the cemetery at Handsworth as she wished to put flowers on her daughter's grave.

Aunty Dolly, as she was known, died tragically after an accident at the age of twenty-two. It seems that she was hit in the ear by a snowball, which developed into meningitis. She was regarded as a saintly person. Having placed the flowers on the grave, my grandmother turned to walk away and said, "Goodbye, my wench." Childlike, I asked, "Why did you say that, Granny?" and she replied, "Well, she was my wench." Her face looked pale, drawn and unbearably sad. Eventually I returned home and told my Mother about this. She told me that Aunt Dolly's funeral procession passed men gathering in the harvest and she and others thought how God had gathered in the harvest with her beautiful soul. She also told of how when she had returned from the funeral, she was broken-hearted and the vicar went in to comfort her. As the vicar departed, the gas man came in to empty the meter. He realised the situation and turning to my grandmother, he said in the kindliest voice, "Remember there are The Everlasting Arms." This unknown stranger brought her great comfort. At a very early age, I had suddenly become acquainted with very great sadness. I knew what it was to look at the face of the broken-hearted.

I was the eldest of the three brothers; my two younger brothers were weak in their early years and somehow they became neglected by the extended family. I found myself regarded with favour, although I felt this was unjust towards my siblings and felt angry at the attitude of others. I had begun to realise that life could be very unfair. I was to discover it could also be very cruel, as further events would show.

It was an afternoon when I was eight years old, sitting at my desk as a member of class standard 3. When the door of the classroom opened for afternoon lessons, the tall figure of the Head Master appeared. He strode across the room to a desk occupied by a small crippled boy who had an iron on his leg. (We knew him affectionately as pudding rice.) He stopped at the boy's desk, and ordered the children around out of their desks. He asked the boy, "Did your parents send you to school this morning?" Yes, said the small boy. "And did you come?" asked the Head Master. "No," said the boy; at this, the Head Master pulled the boy over the desk and severely thrashed him with a cane. The boy screamed in agony. The Head Master not being deterred by the boy's screams, the thrashing continued. When it stopped I saw a quivering body and heard the sound of long heart-rending sobs. It was a spectacle: as young as I was, I would never forget. The classroom teacher was quite impassive to this happening. The Head Teacher had to pass my desk to leave the room; as he passed I sat bolt upright and stared into his face. He went deep red and went out.

So was the unforgettable thrashing of pudding rice.

Weeks later an older boy, for a truly bad misdemeanour, was called out of class at assembly and severely flogged by the same Head Master. The flogging was most severe down his back and legs with the maximum force of the cane. The boy did not shout or cry but towards the end a cry like a wounded animal escaped from his lips. Some hours later in the playground the boy was surrounded by his peers. He was their hero. He became the school bully, and during World War II was an army deserter.

The Head Master, shortly after these events, was to be promoted and given a brand new school in another part of the city. Appreciation of his works was written in the parish magazine, distinguishing him as a builder of good character.

Nemesis, however, was waiting: he shortly afterwards died of cancer of the throat. Much was made of it and sympathy expressed. I felt no pity for him. I could still remember the sobs of poor pudding rice.

In regard to corporal punishment there are those that say it never did them any harm, they should be grateful to God for their powers of endurance. However, they were not small, weak, crippled little children, as was the case of pudding rice. He was one among three or four little children and was loved in his vulnerability; his suffering was our suffering. Quite simply we all loved him.

There was a senior class teacher, a Mr. George, who followed the same teaching examples as the Head Teacher. One day my young brother came home from school and hid his hand under the tablecloth. My Mother, however, saw it.

"Who did this?" Mr. George, he said. "Right," she said, "I will deal with this." She stopped serving dinner, the pinafore was removed and she left the room with haste. She returned later saying she had dealt with it.

My Mother had a vicious Irish temper and when roused her eyes spat fire. Her voice was as unfriendly and destructive as a naval Broadside.

Some ten years later, as a young man, I happened to bump into Mr. George in his retirement. He bumbled his apologies regarding this incident. My Mother, when we were young, would say, "Do not get me in a passion." She knew how dreadful her anger could be.

Mr. George once boasted that he had specially obtained his cane because he knew it would hurt a great deal. Towards the end of his teaching career his cane disappeared, and later I discovered that my sister and her friend had hidden the cane behind a cupboard. Shortly after this he retired.

Small boys in those days often threw stones, often at each other and on one such occasion it happened that a stone hit me on the forehead.

A swelling arose and after two days the swelling enlarged and I could not open my right eye.

My mother said to my father that he must take me to our doctor, about a mile and a half away. After waiting in his waiting room, I was lead through into his surgery. He asked his wife to bring a basin of very hot water; he sat me on a chair for the purpose of lancing the swelling. He plunged the lance in my forehead, twisted it round, and yellow pus poured forth. I nearly fainted; he rushed to the window and opened it quickly. He wiped the wound with hot Borax lint and held it on for a moment, and said to my father that this must be done several times a day. Then came the long walk home. The instructions were duly carried out. To ensure cleanliness, a huge bandage was wrapped round my head with a pad of lint under it.

Monday morning came and I was sent to school. The class teacher was the dreaded Mr. George. After assembly I went to sit at my desk, and, looking up, a strange looking figure stood in front of the class. He was tall, gaunt, and dressed in black. He was the rector of the parish. Before coming to Handsworth, he had occupied an important position at Westminster Abbey. Having seen my bandaged head he walked and sat beside me. He put his arm around my shoulders and asked what the trouble was. In a few words I explained what had happened. I was struck by his great concern and his kindness. His very presence conveyed comfort; unhurried, he left me, and I felt grateful to him. Sometimes I would go for walks around the parish. There was a road named Heathfield Road, named after earlier days. I would look across the Heathfield Estate from a gap in the fencing and I could see James Watt's house; then very dilapidated. I was informed later that the house was dismantled with every brick numbered; it was shipped to America. The importance of this building, in spite of its ruinous state, seemed to be disregarded by those in high authority. Beyond it stood the church, which he had attended and I knew he had taken a great interest in it. This became the last resting place of the three men James Watt, Matthew Boulton, and Richard Murdock, who were the prime movers of the Industrial Revolution. The importance of these men in the history of mankind is today, I feel, much overlooked. These great men whose intelligence and industry changed the history of the world. It seems that there is little emphasis by historians today concerning these men. As a small child I was taken to view the great statue of James Watt as well as smaller sculptures of Matthew Boulton and Richard Murdock. I was never taught the importance of these men and how their lives affected the lives of the whole of mankind. When one considers that Matthew Boulton entertained the Empress Catherine II of Russia as a customer to his house in Soho, this small part of England would bring about enormous changes for the benefit of mankind.

They did not know that they had unleashed a power which would power the railways that would cross-continents; they did not know that he power of steam would allow ships to cross mighty oceans; today the power of steam is mighty in its various applications. In a small building at the side of the enormous Soho factory was invented and made a stream press that produced coins by the thousand.

Half penny coin - front and back.
The original coins are in the possession of the author.

Original copper coins made on the first steam press by Matthew Boulton and James Watt.

Two one pennies - front and back.

Cartwheel coin - front and back.

The commercial world of commerce was thereby revolutionised. Permission to export the steam press was only possible through an Act of Parliament. From Soho came forth other manufacturing goods for the world, from stained glass to trouser buttons. Eventually developers demolished this huge factory. Within walking distance of where this great edifice had stood, I was born. From this corner of England came the beginning of the Industrial Revolution. Soho Road still exists, and in it the house built by Matthew Boulton in which he once entertained the Empress of Russia. A noble past is not entirely forgotten.

Handsworth Church that I knew so well was called the Westminster Abbey of the Midlands. When it became time to appoint a new incumbent, it was considered right to appoint a minor Canon of Westminster Abbey, Daniel Bainbridge. He was to remain incumbent for nineteen years.

At his retirement the local press announced his retirement with words that were not intended for his comfort. The placards in their own words stated he had, "Downed Tools". Although I was small, I heard people talk and reported his unhappiness at the words that they had used. Some said the parish was asleep; this was not so. His wife led the Mothers' Union. Two things I remember; the first was an occasion when she said to the assembled members that there was no excuse for dirtiness in children, as soap was cheap enough. A certain Mrs. Bailey replied from the hall, "Soap costs money and poor people find it difficult to pay." The rector's wife replied, "I did not know you lived in such poverty, Mrs. Bailey." Mrs. Bailey was not to be out-done; she replied, "When I come here, I leave my poverty at home." Mrs. Bailey lived next door to my house and her work at the washtub earned enough money to keep her out-of-work husband and four children. She attended the parish church and during election time, it seemed odd to me that she went from house to house canvasing for the Conservative Party. Eventually her hard work led to a heart attack from which she died in the presence of the clergy from the parish church.

When I was eight years old she sent me a book as a present; it was entitled "The Metaphors of Saint Paul", with a message. It was a birthday present and I would understand the book when I was older. Again, I remember we had a new curate, a certain Mr. Wright, and she spoke to him publicly in a severe tone and said words to the effect she had seen him on the dance floor. His reply was, "I do not have a petticoat government at home; I will not have it here." Mr. Wright became a popular figure in the parish.

There is, in the Tower of Handsworth Church, a peal tablet, which states a full peal was rung to celebrate the wedding of the rector and Mrs. Bainbridge, in 1924. The peal was successful at the third attempt. The conductor of the peal was brought in from Aston Church. The peal was rung by the Sunday Service Ringers, an achievement in the circumstances worthy of praise. The people of the parish I knew felt that the rector and Mrs. Bainbridge were members of the aristocracy and were regarded as such. The front door to the rectory was for private visitors. A separate side door was reserved for parishioners.

I was now in standard 5 class, ten or eleven years of age. In due course Canon Bainbridge was replaced, a clergyman from the parish of Spark Hill was suddenly made the Rector of Handsworth, and he brought with him a lady worker in the form of a Deaconess known as Sister Hannah. Sister Hannah became a visitor to many ladies of the Parish. He, on the other hand, joined the local bowls club and was known as "Canon". His work in the parish was an effort to get men interested in church affairs. He left after three years to take up an important incumbency of a fashionable church in London. Before he left he engaged a curate, one Eric Loveday. Eric Loveday attempted to work with young people and formed a boys' Bible class for Sunday afternoon, which some boys including myself joined.

Benny Ward, my friend, and I approached Mr. Loveday, and asked if we could attend his confirmation class and a date was fixed for us to attend his classes at the Church in the evening. The classes continued for six weeks but when the time came for me to attend the actual confirmation I was taken ill with influenza. Mr. Loveday visited me and agreed I could not be present. My next visitor was Benny Ward who said if he could not go as my friend he would not attend either. We would both wait for another opportunity. I am sure taking into consideration certain following events, in all this lay the hand of God. Eric Loveday gave his last talk to the school when I was about to leave. He said that he had attended a theological college at Oxford, he was proud to have gone there and he mentioned the principal of the college; a great scholar named Dr Major. (Little did he know, or did I know, that the little boy sitting in front of him in short trousers and unkempt clothes would many decades later attend the same college and be invited to supper with the great scholar he had mentioned.) I am proud to still possess a signed book of one of the theological works he gave me.

Eric Loveday left to go to a parish in Smethwick. On a lighter note, Eric Loveday attempted to teach the young people one Christmas to recite the poem, "The Village Blacksmith"; the group could not recite the poem, getting muddled up with the lines of the poem. So to make it easier for the group he advised them to recite the first line, by the people at the front, "Under the spreading chestnut tree, AT THE FRONT"; the second line, "The village Smithy stands, AT THE BACK". This was acceptable in the practice sessions, but when it came to the Christmas Party the group entered the stage and commenced to recite the poem but included the added words "at the front" and "at the back" and all present enjoyed the whole evening, all present enjoyed the fun. Eric Loveday died as he stepped from the plane on a visit to Australia. This occurred just after the Second World War.

When I was about twelve years old, the top classes of the schools were much reduced by pupils being sent to the grammar school. Boys and girls were sent to all sorts of secondary schools for further education. Before this, many children up to age of twelve regularly played in the street. The street, in the eyes of the educationalists, became an entity in its self, from which children received a type of social education. On the other hand, stress was to be placed on children receiving academic qualifications. The street was a place for children, where they met and developed friendships and formed into small groups. Benny (Beresford) Ward and I formed a friendship; he was the eldest of five children and in some ways the weakest. He had very bad eyesight and always wore glasses. At other times others children joined us, such as David Lynol and Frankie Green, in the various things that children got up to in those days.

The "Old Peck" was a piece of waste ground at the end of Putney Road and was used as a rubbish dump by many. Everything could be found there, from old baths to old sewing machines, and all sorts of household rubbish. It was a playground for many children. One day a group of children got together and dug a hole about six feet deep. Then they tunnelled underground a further six feet so that inside it was a dugout (think of the First World War dugouts). One day we were playing in the dugout when we were warned a policeman was in the offing. We scrambled out and hid ourselves where we could see what was happening. A portly policeman approached the entrance to the dugout, stood on the top of it and stamped with all his force but it did not give way. Eventually he gave up and continued on his beat along Putney Road. We all waited until had gone some distance, then from our hiding place we peered at the scene, and to our amazement, white-faced and bespectacled, out of the entrance appeared the head of Benny Ward. He looked very funny and we all roared with laughter. Onto this scene suddenly appeared a lad; he was smaller than us, and he was named Jacky Raybold. He approached us with a serious look on his face and we paused to listen to what he had to say. He said, "My brother has just said to me there is going to be another war; there will be no front line and we shall all be in it, the Germans will take some beating." What he had said, despite our young age was enough to make us think. In due course his words were sadly to prove prophetic.

It was decided by a small group of boys to make what we called "Can Fires"; a tin can was obtained by each of us, mostly treacle tins. Large holes would be pierced in the sides of the tin and a loop of old wire was fastened on top of the tin, and when small bits of wood and coal were lit inside and swung round it seemed like a huge Catherine wheel. We tested our fire cans secretly and found them to work well; when swung round quickly, the greater the fire.

So when evening approached the next night we went down a side street. In one of the houses there lived an old man who was very disapproving of children. We swung our fire cans around with great joy; what fun it was. After about three minutes or so one can broke loose from its sling, and went away high in the air. Its appearance was wonderful, it looked like a comet; but it sped towards the roof of the house where lived the rather disagreeable old man. Over the roof it went and we heard just enough sound to realise it had fallen in his garden. Half a minute later the air was rent as the sounds of his dreadful explosions of expletives, in number and kind such as I had never heard before, poured out in his rage. From our hiding place, after a short time we saw the front door open and he ran into the road. He saw nothing and heard nothing. We had quickly removed the cans of fire. Eventually he returned to his house and all was still and quiet. In the silence we gathered our thoughts and began to realise the stupidity of what we had done. We were fortunate that this episode had not been the subject of more serious trouble. There were no more can fires, they were consigned to the dustbin. We rarely went down that street again. We were growing older and beginning to realise that life had a serious side.

Other children caused amusement; The "Old Peck" was a place where old bicycles and parts of these were thrown away. A fellow named Ernest Clifton collected parts of bicycles until he had sufficient to build a bicycle. He could not, however, find any tyres. He rode this bicycle on an early morning paper round. The noise it made was terrible, something like an army of tanks coming down the road. Then there was the prank the children performed about Billy Whitherington. They spread the rumour that he was dead. They did this by referring to this non-event in the presence of adults. Women used to meet in a local shop, which became noted for gossiping A group of women were there when Mrs Whitherington entered. Four or five women stared at her with sorrowful eyes and expressed their sincere condolences. Mrs Whitherington looked amazed and asked what on earth they were talking about. They said, "It is about your poor Billy, we have heard that he is dead." She replied with some force, "Billy is at home having his breakfast at this moment."

Everybody knew Billy was fond of pigeons but he had no pigeon loft; instead he used a small back bedroom. To loose his pigeons out he would simply open the bedroom windows.

One day about this time we were trespassing on some allotments, when a policeman arrived and decided to take our names. Benny Ward told such a story of having a violent and over strict father. That this policeman was so impressed that we were very relieved when he put his notebook away.

Some groups of children were for street sports; others would form whip and top groups and there was a skipping rope activity where the rope was stretched across from pavement to pavement. Hopscotch beds were made with coloured chalks and in the summer evenings the whole street was alive with children having a very happy time. These were our days of care-free joy. These games came to an end when secondary education began, as children had to wear uniforms and had homework to do, which occupied their attention. The street lost its power.

In some cases a family would refuse to let their children go to the grammar school; my family did; also the Ward family did not allow their children to go. The reasons given were the cost of the school uniform and parents insisting their children went to work. We had one very clever boy named Frederick Sydenham. As a scholar he was brilliant, but he had to follow in his father's trade as a cobbler. The last I saw of him was in his father's shop mending shoes.

Born within a few days of my birth was a girl called Olive Rose, who lived a few houses up the road from me; she with other girls would join in the fun that the street provided. Between the ages of nine and ten I was taken to the fair where there were lions and I saw the actions of the lion tamer. He went into the cage with a ferocious lion, only for a second or two; he had a whip which he used, swinging it in a diagonal movement from his right shoulder to his left foot and from his left shoulder to his right foot. I noticed this; one day Olive Rose and I walked into the back garden of a neighbour's house with the girl who lived there, Joan Elliott. A discussion broke out as to what we wanted to be when we were grown up. With childlike stupidity I said I wanted to be a lion tamer. They looked at me with some amusement. I had a whip in my hand from the whip and top game and so demonstrated how to use it following the pattern of the lion tamer. Olive Rose stood a yard away and worked out in her mind how to dodge the whip. She edged forward little by little, staring me in the face; when very near to me, her hand reached out and grabbed my hand. The look on her face was fearless. I could forget being a lion tamer – I could not tame two little girls. One day, as a birthday present I had a nice new blazer I accidentally tore one of the pockets nearly off. Not knowing what to do, I looked up the road and saw Olive Rose. She was about ten or eleven years of age. I showed her the blazer; she took it off me and went into her house, brought it back and showed me the effort she had made to sew the pocket on. When I went home my Mother saw it and asked who had done this. I told her Olive Rose; she said, "No one teaches girls how to sew these days."

Olive Rose's father was known as Billy Rose, and was admired for his prowess as an excellent swimmer. He died, mortally wounded, in the First World War. Every month a photograph of his little daughter was sent to the front to note her progress. At school we were taken to the baths to learn how to swim. The girls' swimming was completely different to the boys' swimming. When I could swim 150 yards I was informed I need not go again. No one could swim as well as I could. Then one day an assembly was called at school; all the children and teachers were present. A small rostrum was placed in the centre of the gathering, and when all were present the Head Master said he would present Olive Rose with a medal; she had swum one mile. With great applause he pinned a medal on her dress. All had applauded her accomplishment but she looked almost unconcerned. Young as I was, I realised that this girl had a presence difficult to describe. Her father would have been proud to know of her achievements, perhaps in heaven he did. Prayers were said and we went home.

Olive Rose passed for the grammar school. After I was coming home from work, which I had just commenced, I met her by her house. She said that they had taught her at grammar school the correct way to pronounce electricity. She looked very attractive in her new uniform. Olive Rose did not join the church organisations at all. When older she joined a very selective and costly tennis club, married a lucky young man and disappeared. On reflection I realised that she had inherited her father's physical strength. Her mother was known for some time even after her marriage as Florry Porter, and further more as a woman of captivating beauty. These gifts their daughter had inherited. At fifteen years of age she was beginning to bloom. She was a friend of my boyhood and will always be remembered. I was the recipient of her kindness.

When I was fifteen my Grandfather died; he had been a well-known figure and respected by many. My Grandfather was a man of character and to me an example of how to live. I looked on him as a natural leader of men. I felt his wife was a fine lady of great courage and determination. His last position was as an overseer in charge of some three hundred boys at a school run by a board of guardians. This was at the Wigmore School, situated at the edge of West Bromwich, which could be approached across the fields from Handsworth Wood. With the aid of five other men he had to teach the boys the rudiments of agriculture and horticulture. He retired due to ill health and died soon after. His funeral was a large affair. My mother told me she counted thirty-three wreaths. I was named after him, being the eldest grandchild. A few weeks after the funeral my Granny sent for me. She saw me alone and, without emotion, handed me his hunting crop as he had once ridden to hounds. She said to me, without tears, "This is as gold to me." I still have it. She died within a few months, as was her wish. My Grandfather had once told me he had been in bed sixteen weeks with rheumatic fever and although his wife had seven children (only six survived), during that time she took in washing to earn money to provide for the family.

Wheeler Street consisted of two hills, one going down to Farm Street and the other going up to Soho Road. Benny Ward, now fifteen years old, purchased a bicycle and was riding downhill towards Farm Street – his speed was fast. A middle-aged lady was crossing the road.

She stopped a few yards in front of the bicycle, turned round and bent forward, not seeing the speeding bicycle. Benny Ward slammed on both brakes but this did not prevent the front wheel embedding itself in the centre of her rather wide bottom. All was still for a brief second then suddenly she spun round, stood upright and with a very loud voice shouted, "YOU S-D." This was not a place to offend the local populace. The policemen went about in twos in those days. So Benny Ward sped off at great speed to the top of the opposite hill, where he reached safety and was able to tell me about this amusing incident. With the introduction of secondary education, destroying the power of the street, the story of my childhood comes to an end.

My friend Benny Ward and I became interested in bell ringing. We were told by the verger to ask the chief bell ringer, Mr. Danby, if we could be taught bell ringing. Mr. Danby agreed and said we must learn to ring the service bell (one bell rung by itself). When I first entered the belfry I was astonished at what I saw; there were boards recording the peals of famous bell-ringers of the past. I saw in the corner of the belfry a picture of a young man. I was told he had learnt to ring there at Handsworth. This man was a descendant of well-known bell ringers and was known to be so. As time went on I was to learn that he had left ringing at Handsworth and went to ring at Saint Martins in the bullring in the centre of Birmingham, where he became a highly proficient ringer of twelve bells. Later on in life he was invited to ring at Saint Paul's Cathedral in an important memorial peal. In public life, he became Lord Mayor of Birmingham. Here was an unknown history, which intrigued me. Mr. Danby told me a great deal regarding bell ringers of the past. Sometimes after bell ringing practice he encouraged me to walk with him towards his home. His memory went back to 1902, when the men returned from the Boer War. He told me of the grand parade held at the parish church. He also told me of how the shaft of the clapper of the seventh bell broke. "The Regimental Band" preceded the soldiers as they marched into the church accompanied by the ringing of the church bells (they had recently been increased from six to eight). The bell ringers realized that the shaft of the clapper of the seventh bell had broken, thus spoiling the sound of the peal. While the service was being conducted in the crowded church, some of the bell ringers with great effort removed the broken clapper and took it to the nearby forge and the village blacksmith Isaac George, with heat and hammering, welded the shaft of the clapper together. "This had to be carried back to the church tower and replaced in the bell. The whole thing was successfully concluded," he said. When the soldiers came out of the church the full peal of eight bells rang out. The soldiers were dressed in the ragged uniforms they had worn in the Boer War, and it was a striking sight. Along the pavements there were hundreds of people waving and cheering their troops who had come home safely.

One Sunday evening after ringing the service bell, Benny Ward and I went to church for evensong. When the service was over, we and some other young people saw a young clergyman standing near the chancel; we thought he must be the new curate. So we went up four or five together to make our acquaintance with him. He said that he had come to see and be seen. We felt he was very approachable and had a very friendly manner. He did become the curate in place of Mr. Loveday. When he came, the Sunday afternoon Bible class was brought to an end. Instead, he started a Young People's Fellowship in which the boys and girls met together in the church on a Sunday afternoon, but sat separately. He took prayers, we sang hymns, there was a Bible reading, and religious talks. In the week he arranged for a boys' club to be held and also a girls' club with a lady in charge. He arranged young people's parish socials with a dance band in attendance, and church life for young people quickened considerably. He started a confirmation class. I was now sixteen and, with Benny Ward and others, joined the new curate's confirmation classes in church. His approach to the subject was different to what we had known before. His first talk was on the meaning of life. What had we been born for? What were we going to do with our lives? As time went on, he saw each one of us separately. He enquired about our prayer life as to what we did. I told him how I said my prayers in bed at night, and went into detail. He seemed amazed, as I had done this without instruction. I feel that he had prayed for me as I had prayed for him. When the time came for the confirmation service, I felt honoured to be confirmed by the then bishop of Birmingham, Dr E.W. Barnes. Benny Ward was confirmed with me.

My parents ordered me to go and help our milkman in the slums of Birmingham every Saturday morning. I did this for only two or three months, but I shall never forget the experiences or some of the things I saw among the desperately poor. It was a Christmas morning I went to one home where there was a lady and three little children, all badly dressed and not very clean. In one corner of the room was a large box of apples. She had not seen her husband for a few days, and said, pointing to the apples, "That is my children's Christmas dinner." She had no money to pay for the milk, so I just left it.

I had been up very early that morning and it was a long walk to the milk round, and therefore a long walk to return home. I returned home feeling very tired and opened the back door to go into the house. I was met with the Christmas dinner being cooked. I walked in and quite simply, while my Mother was cooking the dinner in the next room, I broke down and wept. As I was young and sensitive I thought of the pathos and the injustice of the scene.

On another occasion I walked down the street and passed a court, which consisted of back-to-back houses formed in a square with a midden in the middle. The whole place was crowded. A hearse drew up in the far distant corner of the court, a door opened and on the step there stood a frail old lady dressed in black with a walking stick. Absolute silence fell, she stepped forward and the large crowd parted to enable her to slowly walk to the hearse. Royalty could not have been more respectfully treated. The whole crowd, though uneducated and poverty stricken, were moved by some deep spiritual presence. I was struck by the complete and utter silence and the reverence shown to the old lady by people of all ages. I felt the presence of a great spiritual power and words are inadequate to describe such an awe-inspiring sight. I felt privileged to witness such an event. Its memory will remain with me forever.

Chapter 2

When I left school the first task was to find work. I obtained a Birmingham newspaper and looked at the situations vacant. In the whole of Birmingham there were three vacancies for young people, miles from where I lived. So I decided to walk the streets in the factory areas and look for work. I set off towards Aston and found a road with my name on it – Fredrick Road. It was then that I met a friend of mine, George Perks. He attended the grammar school called King Edwards Aston Grammar School, although why he attended this one instead of the local one I could never understand. He told me there was a clever boy in his class; he was clever because he could play the oboe. His name was Enoch Powell.

Having walked the length of Fredrick Road I looked across the road and saw a small factory; it said on a billboard, boy wanted. They said they were mathematical instrument makers. It said "Engine dividing done". I applied and got the job at seven shillings and sixpence a week. I worked at this firm who employed intelligent and very nice people. When the great depression came (they stopped building the Queen Mary) my pay was reduced to four shillings and sixpence per week. This being so, I needed a better-paid job.

So I took the worst job I ever had, which was as an aluminium caster. The work was in heat and dangerous; health and safety had not been thought of. People I knew asked me why one side of my face was red, I said that was the side nearest the furnace. The work was called "Slush Casting"; molten metal was poured into a mould using a ladle and then back into the ladle, then into the furnace. This required care and skill. Occasionally shoes and clothes were splattered with molten metal. One day a fellow put his ladle that had become wet into the molten metal. The whole thing exploded and the metal seemed to cover him from head to foot. He shook himself violently; we rushed to his aid. I thought that the metal would run into his shoes so I pulled them off quickly. He was then taken to hospital; after a few days he recovered and was back at work. A few days later I attended a missionary meeting at church and saw how missionaries had organised young men of a foreign country to learn how to use typewriters. At the meeting I looked at my hands; they were gnarled and blistered due to my work. It was time to make a move. I had been constantly advised to leave this job, this I eventually did. I got a job at the General Electric Company at Whitton as a storekeeper.

In the job I was put in charge of a store. I shall never forget going into the large engineering works. There I saw huge pieces of machinery being made. There were big pieces of steel, several feet long, on enormous lathes being machined by serious looking men. These would eventually go to power stations for the production of electricity. I was taken to the store over which I was to take charge. The work was mostly clerical but the change from my previous work was immense.

It was part of my duties, towards the end of the working day, to collect micrometers and gauges and to take them for safekeeping to my store. In the course of going round the workshops I saw machinery that amazed me. This was before the days of computer use. I was surprised to see machines that performed complex operations automatically, without human control; also I was full of admiration for the men who showed high skill. I remember seeing a turner at his lathe making an enormous bolt, which had a double buttress thread. The design of such an object must have demanded high intelligence. What must not be forgotten was the great ability and skill of the men who machined and produced such articles. These men I knew had no formal higher education to speak of; yet they performed their task with remarkable efficiency.

Occasionally I had to visit the tool room in order for micrometers and gauges to be inspected and if necessary, readjusted. The men in the tool room were very highly regarded by the other workers. In order to attain personal respect when I visited the tool room, I removed my warehouse coat and wore normal clothes – a privilege usually accorded to people of staff position. I received from the tool room an article that caused some concern for the operative. I looked at the drawing concerned and I judged that there was something wrong. I decided to take it back to the senior toolmaker who had made it, with the accompanying drawing. I entered the tool room with some trepidation and went to the man concerned and placed the article on his bench. He stared at me almost in disbelief. I then said, without realising what the effect would be, that there had been a mistake. First his eyes seemed to bulge with a mixture of anger and contempt. I shall never forget his reaction in an incredulous and exceptionally loud voice; he shouted the word "mistake". Then again the word "mistake", at the full power of his voice. Then he said, very loudly, "We do not make mistakes here." Other workers turned their heads at the sound of his anger. I placed the drawing concerned on his bench; he looked at it, then at me, and in a few seconds pointed out how I had misread the drawing. I expressed regret at causing such trouble, gathered the necessary articles up and departed. I did not feel the least bit upset by people shouting at me from my early youth. I had always regarded this as a sign of their weakness. The man's appearance and his actions I somehow felt most amusing. The few times I told this story to others it caused amusement.

One day in front of the door to my store, on a sloping ramp, a machine weighing several tons had been placed. So that it would not fall, a huge rope was tied to a great stanchion. To get into my store I walked in front of it, and opened the door to walk in; as I did so, the rope broke. I realised how near I had been to a dreadful death. The whole building shook violently, people ran. The uppermost thought in my mind was, "Why has my life been spared?" I felt I was needed for some purpose. I felt I had been the object of prayers from someone somewhere.

A Mr. Wilson ran the boys' club. He had planned one evening we would have a debate. The subject: "Capital Punishment". He chose five lads including me to lead the debate, by each giving a speech on the subject. I went to the local library and found books on capital punishment and read them. By doing this preparation I was ready to give a speech. When evening came, we five boys stood in front of the assembled club and each in turn gave his speech. I spoke last. Mr. Wilson, after I had finished speaking, turned to the assembled group, and said, "There is only one here who knows how to speak in public." He seemed to take due note of my ability and there were no more debates.

Not long afterwards Mr. Wilson decided to have an open-air youth meeting at which two people belonging to his club would speak. The subject was "The need for Christianity in life". I and another spoke and we were well received.

The whole event was regarded as a success. This occurred in Handsworth Park at the bandstand.

Handsworth Park in my childhood and early youth was a happy hunting ground. Most residents some time or other spent time in Handsworth Park. It was properly named Victoria Park. Many events connected with Birmingham took place in this park. Once a year Pat Collins of Walsall brought his enormous fair to the park. It boasted of many important rides, especially what was referred to as the dragon ride. This was a very fine fair ground organ and the whole event was well attended and went on until late at night. The fair ground steam traction engines were large and magnificent. On one occasion I showed so much interest in one named "Goliath" that the driver offered me six pence to drive it round the fair ground under his guidance. I was only twelve years old so I refused his kind offer; with hindsight I have regretted it ever since.

In this spot a few years later I gave my first address in public. The park had small wooded slops that in our early days became Sherwood Forest. We carved our initials on stout trees. We were told that Albert Ketelbey, a well-known composer of the day, used to walk from his house in South Road and sit on a bench in the park and was seen to be playing his invisible piano. From where he probably sat, it was meadowland as far as Handsworth Church Tower, where bells had been rung for some centuries. Possibly he recalled their sound when he composed his piece "Bells across the

Meadow". One can imagine memories of Handsworth Park would be in the minds of many men who left to serve in the Forces in various parts of the world. Many of these did not return.

Indeed, when Handsworth Bells were recast in 1955, one bell had the inscription "He did not return". I knew this referred to a young man, a slight acquaintance of mine, who served in the Royal Navy. I knew his parents and that he was their only child.

My brothers and sister knew what it was to spend happy hours in the park. Handsworth Park had a double railway line running through it; it was this that enthralled us to know some brief moments of intense excitement. All between the ages of eight to eighteen stood by the railings to see the Mid-Compound pass through. It would thunder its way through twice a day. We saw this mighty engine with its chocolate coloured boiler, the piston rods moving at unbelievable speed, then the highly polished connecting rods as they flashed in the sunlight. Then there were the wheels over six feet in height pounding the rails. Yet it was the wonderful sound we heard, the hissing of steam, but overall was the ear-splitting rhythmic sound from the smoke stack. With its sight and sound we felt we were in the presence of a most wonderful mechanical monster. It seemed to be alive, full of sound and movement. I once saw the face of the engine driver, it was very white with black oil stains across his face; but his eyes were small and dark and full of intense concentration as he peered through the small glass window. The train sped through the nearby tunnel as we waited to hear the sound of its whistle. The last train ran in 1971.

When I was approximately the age of twenty I saw six or seven eighteen-year-old lads talking together on the cricket pitch. They looked solemn and serious. They had been called up to join the military and had to go for six months training in the army. Everyone felt this was because of a coming war. A few years afterwards, I had been invited to dinner by a prosperous businessman who had told me he had been called up into the military; now approaching old age, he had tried to find others he had been with, but so far he could not find one. My young brother Gordon joined the church choir where he obviously took note of the many sermons he had heard. We had a friend, David Lynall, whose father had died in the First World War. David died suddenly and unexpectedly of pneumonia, which was a shock to us all. My mother told us of his death at the dinner table. We sat shocked and stunned. My brother, looking across the table at me, said quietly, "They go to somewhere better." His time as a choirboy had given him faith.

My next public speaking was arranged by the deanery and had older men than myself to speak. A huge concourse of young people met in Handsworth Park. I addressed the people gathered, and it was a great experience and a success. Three lads and two girls decided that we would hold a church service every Sunday evening in Lent at a church hall in the Hockley district. Both girls could play the piano so it was useful for hymn singing. We advertised the event and turned up to take the service about 6pm one Sunday night. About 30-40 children up to the age of twelve turned up. We found it difficult to keep order and could not make ourselves heard. A very old lady walked in, and from that time onwards there was no trouble. We taught the children to sing choruses, which they enjoyed. When we left on the last Sunday evening they surrounded our bus and sang, "I will make you fishers of men." We felt we had done a worthwhile job.

Following this, a fellow and I were chosen by Mr. Wilson to join a team for a mission at Sparkhill. This was led by an International Evangelist, Gypsy Smith, and necessitated, as members of the team, attendance at training for the course. While training one Saturday afternoon we were privileged to hear a fine sermon by the Provost of Birmingham Cathedral at that time. The task allotted to us did not in any way involve speaking to people in large numbers. Instead we had to present the Christian message to people in small groups; nonetheless it was a worthwhile experience.

The time came for Mr. Wilson to leave and go to an important parish in London, but only as a curate. His last talk to the young people's fellowship ended with the words, "I came that ye should have life and have it more abundantly." He had certainly done this and there are many young people who would owe him a great debt of gratitude, including myself.

As I slowly progressed with my church bell ringing I came in contact with others, some about my own age. Ernest Lewis became a bell ringer at Handsworth and was an apprentice joiner. He was physically strong. Another bell ringer was Sidney Holloway who lived in Smethwick, which was not far away. Sid was slightly older than me but his upbringing was very different. He had been privately educated; he had never been a street child. When I first knew him he was at college learning to be a chemist. From him, we learnt things without knowing it. He said he would conduct a peal on the bells at Stone in Worcestershire. He chose Ernest Lewis and myself; it would take about three hours. Peal ringing places a very great strain on the conductor. It requires a faultless memory and great concentration. However we were successful and the peal was completed. Afterwards we descended from the belfry and I saw on the wall of the tower a huge plaque, which recorded that in the early sixteenth century a John Oldnall had left to the parish of Stone twenty pounds a year forever. Another Oldnall had been there centuries before me…

Peal records of the Worcestershire Association of Change

Ringers 1933.

2122. STONE, WORCESTERSHIRE.

On Sunday, May 28, 1933, in Two Hours and Forty-seven Minutes.

AT THE CHURCH OF ST. MARY.

A Peal of Grandsire Doubles, 5040 Changes.

Forty-two six-scores, with ten callings.　　　Tenor 5½ cwt.

*Frederick H. Oldnall	... Treble	*Frederick W. Burnell	4
†Frederick J. Austin	... 2	Sidney O'C. Holloway	5
†Ernest G. Lewis	... 3	Alfred Jones	... Tenor

Conducted by S. O'C. Holloway.

* First peal at first attempt. † First peal. Conductor's first peal as conductor, and first peal of Doubles. Rung in honour of the 85th birthday of Col. Howard, of Stone, Vicar's warden for 60 years.

Peal record of the Worcestershire Association of

Change Ringers 1993.

i.e. a pearl is in an oyster / a pearl refers to a peal of bells

A young clergyman named Mr. Harrison took Mr. Wilson's place, and tried very hard to continue his work.

There are some incidents that one can never forget. In the centre of Birmingham lived a man named James George. He was an expert bell-ringer on heavy bells, and was known throughout the country. I had two friends with whom I sometimes rang in Worcester country villages. One day we went to Worcester Cathedral to a bell ringing meeting, hoping to ring on the bells there. We knew that they were the fifth heaviest set of ringing bells in the world. We had made up our minds to ring only the very lightest bells.

The easiest way to ring bells is down the scale, lightest to the heaviest. There are a few bell-ringers who only get that far in their ringing life. When invited to, we each took a rope of a lighter bell. I took my rope and was ready to ring, then I looked across the spacious belfry and in the far corner, where fell the rope of the heaviest bell (about two and a half tons), an altercation was taking place. A boy no more than fifteen years old stood there; in short trousers, his socks falling about his dirty shoes, his knees none too clean. Two grey-haired, tall, slim men were talking to him and he to them. Eventually these two gentlemen to my amazement seemed to give him the opportunity to ring the very heavy bell. To do this he had to mount a box, which he did. To ring the bell it was necessary to pull the rope, which would pull the bell. When the ringing commenced he would have to do as the others and pull the bell off its upright balance. The two men looked up at him as if help was required; after all, two and a half tons was up there. He slowly shook his head. The signal was given for the ringing to commence; I had to concentrate on what I was doing, as ringing requires great skill. However I managed to glance across the belfry to see what was happening, and there he was ringing this bell with very great ability. His part in the ringing could only be described as perfect. After three or four minutes the ringing was stopped. I wondered how he would re-set the bell in order to make it safe. This is a point where often things go wrong. But he did this, notwithstanding the weight of the bell, in a perfect manner. His task completed, he remained on the box for a second or so and looked across at my companions and me, then jumped off the box and smiled at us. We wondered why he was eventually given permission to ring. We thought James George must have, in spite of his age, trained him. We saw him afterwards and learned he was living, as was Mr. George, in the centre of Birmingham. His name was John Lindon. A few years later when my studies had ceased, owing to the war, I went to St Martins in the Bull Ring and climbed the long staircase to the belfry. I opened the door and in front of me stood a fairly tall youth, well groomed and finely dressed. I recognised him by his shining brown eyes, and his dark curly hair. He greeted me with a handshake. John Lindon had grown up.

The next year I visited Worcester Cathedral again, to attend a meeting of bell ringers. I arrived at the town and made my way to the Cathedral, entered its great doors and walked up the nave. I found when I reached the transept I was a few feet behind an important person; he was old, well dressed. He had a small number of companions around him. I realised I was walking near to Alderman Pritchett DLC, the recorder of Lincoln and a person who held high office in Freemasonry. I felt the men around him probably belonged to that ancient order. He hesitated for a moment then to his left appeared another figure; it was the dean, slightly shorter in stature, slightly bald with a face round and somewhat red. I shall never forget how they met; their eyes shone as they greeted each other, hands on each other's shoulders and with faces full of immense joy.

Then from Alderman Pritchett came the words, "Have you raddled your floor this morning?" With these words both men broke into hilarious laughter. Their actions on the whole seemed like men who had known a happy childhood together. Afterwards Alderman Pritchett talked to his companions about his exploits as a bell ringer in previous years. I had an instant personal reaction to what I had seen and heard. This man, highly esteemed by his fellows, had uttered such words as to indicate his knowledge and appreciation of the hard work performed by the lowly scullery maid. I felt that such a mind indicated a spirit that reached the sublime.

The afternoon ended with a free sumptuous tea. I heard a description of it as "knife and fork".

I thought of the events of the day as I travelled back to Birmingham, not as before on a bicycle, but in the comfort and convenience of a Midland Red bus.

The rector of the parish of Handsworth, the Reverend Canon Lyon, was made Archdeacon of Loughborough thus creating a vacancy of incumbency in the parish. At first it was rumoured that he would be replaced by a returning overseas bishop. After a time, the rumours proved to be true, and one Saturday afternoon I attended the induction of the Right Reverend J.H. Linton as rector of Handsworth; he had for some years been a bishop in Persia. I was tenty years of age. He proved to be an outstanding person; he was a brilliant preacher and a good organiser. It was with his encouragement I decided that I would study with a view to being ordained. I hoped I would matriculate and go to university. The preparation would take three years. I decided to study by correspondence courses. I had help from my many grammar school friends, one especially in mathematics. The subjects I studied provided me with an excellent education that would be of great use to me for the rest of my life. My knowledge of Latin would be of special use in later years when I studied theology. My basic education was such that I could hold my own when I went to the theological college at Oxford. This curtailed many of my other activities; even my bell ringing had almost to cease. The skills I had learnt would stand me in good stead. By October 1939 I considered I was ready to go to London to sit for the London matriculation examination, so I obtained the necessary papers and applied. These were returned to me in early September, saying the examination was cancelled due to declaration of war. Bishop Linton was saddened by my misfortune, and said that, "I would find it difficult one day to reach a state of readiness again." The thought was that three years study had not produced its intended result. My future was unknown and unpredictable; most of my friends at this time were directed into the services. I was next directed to work in a factory on war work. The factory specialised in engineering and required its work force to work to very fine limits. I was ordered to work as a precision grinder. I was given a micrometer and half an hour to learn my new job. I had to work to one thousandth of an inch. Standing for hours a day I found very unpleasant. So after a week or so I volunteered to join the army. Just before I left this firm, when having our mid-day meal, the chief millwright told us, as we ate our sandwiches, that he had been a Regimental Sergeant Major on a troop ship in the First World War. He added that the RSM can go anywhere on the ship, this I remembered.

Chapter 3

World War II began on the 3rd September 1939 and many others listened to the speech by Neville Chamberlain. The first to be called up in my family was my brother Gordon; he was put in the Royal Engineers. My other brother Bernard had already joined the Royal Navy. I was first required to have a medical examination and then was called up to join the Royal Army Ordinance Corps. On the 17th October 1940, I was, with other several young men, called to attend an army barracks for initial training. I was issued with a railway ticket to go from Birmingham to Lichfield. I found myself with other young men in army trucks being taken to Whittington Barracks, Lichfield. I knew, long ago, that Handsworth had provided soldiers of the volunteers which had formed a service battalion of the South Staffordshire Regiment. This later became part of the Territorial Army. The first sight of a barrack room is very depressing, as it contained only the barest of essentials. We were allotted a bed on which we sat and waited. Each one of us joined a queue to collect our army clothes, which included two uniforms. The man who followed me came from Glasgow and sounded very bad tempered and did nothing but grumble. We then returned to our barrack rooms and were told to put on our uniforms in the correct manner. The purpose of the initial training period was to change men from being civilians to soldiers. The length of training was to be six weeks. This period was short as it was wartime. Service life is not a normal life at all. What happened then was typical in the life of many young men. All the men were strangers to each other and it felt very peculiar to sleep in a room with thirty other men. Even the bed felt strange. One's private life had gone. One simple aim remained: to survive. There was always the humorous person who by all sorts of means kept us all happy. A sergeant entered the room and proffered cigarettes from a packet of twenty. A fellow named Walker, emaciated in appearance, said to the sergeant, "Not the whole packet sergeant, just one." It was realised we had a comedian amongst us. Later on, when night approached, Private Walker removed all his clothes and, stark naked, pulled on his long woollen underpants and them alone. He placed his feet in his large boots unlaced; put his steel helmet on his head. In this scanty garb he placed a rifle on his shoulder and marched up and down the centre of the barrack room. The whole place erupted with laughter. He then, in the midst of the laughter, commenced to march the goose step and did a comic version of the Hitler salute. This caused more laughter. The change in the atmosphere was unexpected. Lights out came and we all went to our beds.

Then men began to sing due to the atmosphere created by the previous incident. The songs sung were bawdy, which I had never heard before. I knew men in an adverse situation would gel together and become comrades. Adversity makes strange bedfellows, in this case it most certainly did.

The next day we were ordered into a single queue for inoculations. At the front of the line stood a Medical Officer with his medical equipment spread out on a table at his side. I was next in line to our humourist Walker. As we approached the table he shouted, "I've seen the needle, it is six inches long." A fellow near to me drew the attention of the orderly and said, "Can I be excused as I suffer from appendicitis and have had it several times?" We all laughed, even the M.O. laughed. After all being vaccinated, we were excused duties. For me, I was ordered to see the regimental dentist for teeth extraction. When I went back to the barrack room I looked a sorry state so much so that a young fellow from the Black Country said he would stand in for me and do my duty of fire watching. The next thing that occurred, we were all ordered into the gymnasium. In the course of the exercise I collapsed and was sent to see the army doctor. He ordered that until further notice, I should do more work in the gym. The reason being I was in too low a physical condition. This was due of course to the years of study. The Medical Officer, when I told him of the course, he understood; he was very kind to me. Naturally this did not prevent me, at the end of the six-week Infantry Training Course, having to take part in a twenty-five mile route march. This I managed very well. After this I, and the others, would be ready to leave the Infantry Training Course. This course was very detailed and we learnt much about the way an army is organised. We were also told how great care was taken in the choosing of officers being given high authority and what their duties were. This course ended with a written examination, which I passed.

The next thing that happened, a train took us, complete with all our equipment, to a place called Chilwell near Nottingham. On our arrival we were marshalled in platoons on a parade ground. I was at the front of a platoon, and after a few minutes of waiting a Colonel appeared in front of us, with some junior officers. With a voice just loud enough to be heard by all of us, he welcomed us. His word and demeanour were very obviously those of a well-educated gentleman. He was obviously a person of distinction. The Company Sergeant Major who had accompanied us from Whittington stood with us. The Colonel noticed the man's much-worn uniform and I heard him say to a junior officer, in a low voice, "Take that man to the tailor's shop and have him fitted with a new uniform." After that we were given a meal and sent to a half-built barracks. We were put in a large room with a well-polished wooden floor; there were no beds or blankets. That was where we were expected to sleep, which we attempted to do. After a short time, even though it was "after lights out", the light was suddenly put on and in the door way stood a Sergeant Major, he said jokingly, "Is there an Oldmoore here?" I shouted back, "You probably mean me Sir, my name is Oldnall." He said I had to go to the Medical Officer for examination. The M.O asked how I felt; I told him I felt well. I was then taken outside to join a platoon of men with one missing. I was ordered to take the missing man's place. The missing man had night blindness. Later, I was informed that the men I had left behind were put on a troop ship, which was torpedoed and sank. We were then marched to a railway station at Nottingham. It was extremely dark and we wondered where we were going. We boarded a train and were taken approximately twenty to thirty miles down the line. We disembarked in total darkness. Suddenly a Second Lieutenant appeared and we had to follow him to an ordinance depot very much in its infancy. It did not have any gates; we had to sleep in a newly built room, which contained about thirty beds with blankets. We were the first men in the Army to arrive at this place. We wondered what on earth our duties would be. . It seemed that we were there only to mount guard. It was then that one of our number, a fellow named Hinchley, went absent with out leave (A.W.O.L), to see his wife as she was about to give birth to their baby. A Major was in charge of our unit now, and Hinchley was put on a charge and had to appear before the Major. One soldier marched each side of him; I was one of the soldiers. He was paraded in front of the Major in his office. I was asked about his conduct when he returned to the unit. I said, "His manner was faultless." The Major then for punishment ordered him to be reprimanded, and he immediately carried out the sentence. When this was over he asked the man why he thought he had been dealt with so leniently. He replied, "It is Christmas, Sir." The Major just nodded and the whole matter was concluded.

We continued our duties of mounting guard until eventually the place had expanded with building work and more personnel arrived. This process went on for two years as the number of soldiers increased, a large new camp was built and it housed a large contingent of Auxiliary Territorial Service girls, (A.T.S.) and their officers. In order to keep up morale an entertainments officer was appointed and given certain special duties, such as organising a large band that could be used for military purposes or as a dance band. I was given the job of looking after and taking care of the band's music. I also helped in the small library we had.

During this time, while home on leave, the news was received that my brother had been killed in Greece. This was a dreadfully sad time for us all. I called to mind seeing him off at the railway station and when he was in the carriage, shaking his hand and wishing him good-bye.

I did not know I would never see him again. The memory of this event still fills me with sorrow. The knowledge of my sad news had already reached my unit, when I returned from my leave. I was surprised at the kindly attitude of some of the men and officers to me.

One of the most important dates in British history was 1942. It was then that the battle of El-Alamein was fought and won, bringing much needed victory to the allies. It was decided that the ban on bell ringing should for a very short time be lifted. I applied for permission to go to Leicester to ring. I went to Saint Margaret's Church with its fine peal of twelve bells. I was the only one there in uniform; I grasped the rope of the fourth bell and saw a lady hold the rope of the third bell. This sort of ringing was for those with advanced experience and I was surprised when the ringing commenced. It was excellent. I thought of a speech by a great bell ringer, one high in public life, who said in his speech that to hear bells well rung one had to go to St Paul's Cathedral or St Martins Birmingham. How wrong he was; the ringing was wonderful to listen to and I returned to my unit a happy man indeed.

This is how I felt at that time. As days went by I had time to reflect. A great battle had been won, but what of the cost? I remember reading of how Napoleon, after a great victory, had ridden between the lines of the dead and burst into tears. Wilfred Owen's poem, "Anthem for Doomed Youth", begins with a line about bells. "What passing bells, for those who die as cattle". No other poem begins to me with a line so salutary as this. Even bells of sadness and death would mean nothing to those killed. Victory is only for the living; there is no victory for the departed. The memories of them are both precious and heartbreaking. Their legacy lies in tears from those who loved them and tragically they would never, never have had it so.

So my story continues.

Then I remember my brother Gordon's serious face across the dinner table and hear his voice say, "They go to somewhere better." I believe the soul is indestructible. The line from a hymn states, "From the ground there blossoms red like that shall endless be". The ancient words of the twenty third psalm, "Shall dwell in the house of the Lord forever".

This, as a military organisation, was growing in strength and purpose. Extra personnel were drafted in; this went on over two years, and during this time I passed examinations and became a first class technical clerk in ordnance. It was noticeable that certain companies of men disappeared, having been sent for overseas service. During this period I recall certain events that happened. I state below some of those I still remember.

A young man was ordered to do sentry duty

and when the guard was formed he attempted to shoot the Regimental Sergeant Major in charge, but missed. The R.S.M shouted at him, "You missed me." The soldier then attempted to shoot himself but was only wounded and taken to hospital. The chaplain visited him and told me he had a good university degree and he was somewhat sympathetic towards him. One or two Officers but no men faced a Court Martial for various forms of embezzlement. One wealthy Officer was defended by the finest defence lawyer in the country and was found not guilty. A Sergeant Major in the pioneer corps was Court Martialled for stealing; he was reduced to the ranks. A certain Major I knew in civilian life had been an auditor. One day I saw him going into the Chief Ordnance Officer's Office with a bundle of books dealing with the accounts under his arm, what was said I do not know. The next day a Lieutenant Colonel and the Lieutenant's personal assistant, who was a staff sergeant, and a civilian lady who was the assistant to the latter, had simply disappeared. It was obvious as to why, I knew there were regulations that stated that public scandal had to be avoided and so nothing more was known of the matter.

I was eventually transferred to the company headquarters of the unit. I shared accommodation with the boy who played in the regimental band. They used to play for dances in a large shed, part of which had been converted into a dance hall. I was in the hut waiting for them to return from a dance and I could hear the music in the distance coming towards its end. I heard the national anthem played; when the last note sounded, I heard the loud sound of an explosion. After a few minutes the whole place seemed alive with Officers and those in authority going into various huts demanding that everybody's belongings were to be searched – nothing was to be hidden. When the bandsmen came into the hut eventually, I heard the whole truth: a certain Staff Sergeant Gibbs had been murdered. The day before this happened, I had seen him in the rest room and had spoken to him. The murdered man was a womaniser and was unpopular with the men under him; it seems a certain young man had taken a great dislike to him. This young man had shown a hand grenade to some of his colleagues, and announced he had a present for "Gibby", so at the end of the dance as Gibby left the hall with a lady friend a grenade was thrown from the rear of him. In simple terms it blew his head off; the lady was untouched. The Officer responsible for security called to two soldiers to pick up the body and remove it; they both fainted. The perpetrator of the crime was arrested and handed over to the civil police. They questioned him as to how he acquired the hand grenade, which had been kept in a brick built ammunition store with seven Yale locks. In front of the questioning officer, he bent to the ground, picked up a rusty nail, and demonstrated how he had opened each of the seven locks in turn. A Mr Justice Clarke presided at his trial and he was sentenced to twelve years imprisonment. A friend of mine, Arthur Ward (brother of Benny Ward), walked across the beach on D-day plus three and was instantly blown to pieces. I often think of his fate and compare it to the young man sitting safely in his prison cell.

I was suddenly transferred to "B" company, which consisted of men doing high-grade clerical work. I was no longer excused guard duties and such like. One night I was on guard duty, something I had not done for two or three years. Whilst standing on guard at the main gate I saw the colonel in charge of the establishment driving his large Humber car towards me. I knew that I should have to present arms as a form of salutation. With the greatest of difficulty, I remembered how to do this; I finished the manoeuvre with a stony face forward and a heavy stamp of the right foot. As he passed me, he saluted me. I felt very relieved. Next day I was relieved of all duties.

One day something happened that seemed strange. I heard that a soldier had been put on a charge for losing his cap; he was a person I felt in some way unable to understand. I was in the library when he suddenly appeared to see me. He said he wished to speak to me in confidence. No one else was present. He asked me several questions about my education, and myself; he even asked me the sort of people I had mixed with. I told him I was a church bell ringer and as such I mixed with and kept the company of all sorts. One man I mentioned was a Doctor of Common Law (D.C.L), and also men who held high positions in their various fields. He then asked me to give him my honest opinion of the Commanding Officer of the Battalion and also of his second in command. He mentioned a few others, which I am unable to remember. Then he asked my opinion of the Chief Ordinance Officer, who was a senior officer over all. This position had its name altered after a time and as such became known as the Commandant. I told him again honestly what I felt: that he was an excellent choice for the position. A week later I received a letter with a London postmark on it. Inside I found a copy of Hansards, which is a copy of the House of Commons speeches. It contained an important speech about church bells. This copy of Hansards was signed and dated, and remains in my bell-ringing memorabilia. What I felt was mysterious was the fact that some of these high-ranking officers were replaced, but not the Chief Ordinance Officer. Two or three weeks after this had happened, I was walking past a building and looking inside I could see three or four high ranking officers with this man in front of them in an officer's uniform, now talking in a forceful and serious manner. Having seen this I decided that it was best not to be seen. I have made several guesses as to what sort of position this man held. The real mystery is when there were a thousand men stationed at this place, why he should choose to speak to me. This is a mystery to me and will always be so.

By this time everyone was aware that preparations had to be made for the invasion of Europe. I suddenly found myself belonging to a large company of men, all of whom were receiving special training. We had to learn all sorts of things from how to use a Tommy gun to how to take to pieces a German mine. We were told we were the 21st army group reserves. Our training ended with a written examination. I passed this but few others did. In many ways, a lack of enthusiasm among the men could be seen and felt. Eventually, they were asked as to what the reason was for this. They said that the war would soon be over; of course they were very wrong. The war lasted for another two years. This large group of men was eventually divided up and parcels of men were shipped abroad to various places. I was sent home on leave in preparation for being sent abroad. By this time my home address had changed. This was because my parents had been bombed out in Birmingham. My father had accepted a job as head gardener for a titled family; a house came with his new position. This was a fortunate turn of events, as the family he worked for were very kind. When I returned to my company, I was sent to Liverpool and put on a troop ship, the Duchess of Bedford; none of us there knew our destination. We were all strangers to each other. As the ship sailed away I saw the two Liver Birds slowly disappear. How the others felt I do not know, but I was leaving my country, the future unknown. My heart was in my boots.

One human incident did occur when the ship was about two hundred yards from the quay; a sudden silence fell for a moment. A strong voice was heard to shout, "Shan't be around tomorer." Thus the ship began its journey, taking a large contingent of men abroad. I felt the ship was overcrowded; there were five settings for meals. My bed was a hammock, which I found quite comfortable.

The Duchess of Bedford:
Built 1928 at Glasgow by John Brown & Co. Ltd.
1928 January 24 launched
1928 June 1, maiden Liverpool-Quebec-Montreal
1939 Became a troopship

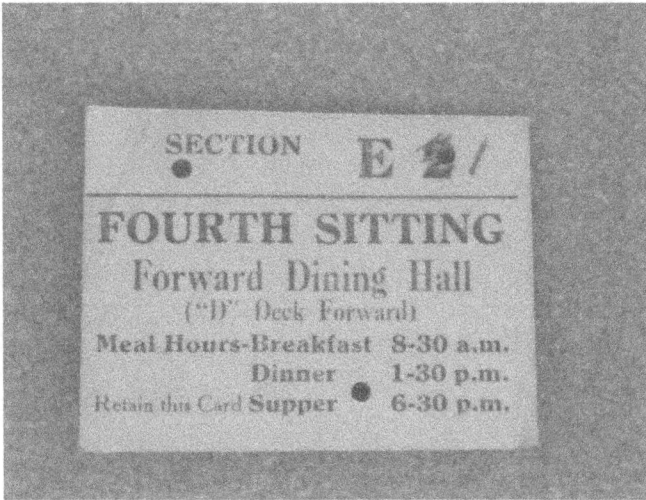

SECTION E 2/

FOURTH SITTING

Forward Dining Hall
("D" Deck Forward)

Meal Hours-Breakfast 8-30 a.m.
Dinner 1-30 p.m.
Retain this Card Supper 6-30 p.m.

A considerable number of personnel had to be fed. I was on the
fourth sitting. Organisation was excellent.

Chapter 4

We passed Gibraltar at midnight; I knew somewhere there was my youngest brother who was in the Navy. We went on in convoy into the Mediterranean Sea. In the morning I went on deck and looked at the sea. The Mediterranean was blue and beautiful. I saw the North Africa Coast. North Africa had already been the scene of the battle of El-Alamein. I thought it was the last resting place of so many British soldiers who had fought and died there. It looked a lifeless sight, inhospitable and foreboding. To keep up morale, films were shown. These had to take place with the temporary use of the officers' ward room. On one occasion when the film ended, I was immediately put on guard of the room. I was told no one was to enter except a naval officer. A naval officer stood by the door; a soldier approached me saying he had left his lifebelt in the wardroom. What should he do? I whispered to him quietly, "Slip in and get it." The naval officer heard me and shouted I had disobeyed orders. I waited until he had finished his tirade, stood to attention and maintained silence. I then remembered that while working in a factory a man had said to me he had been a ship Regimental Sergeant Major in the First World War. He had uttered the all-important words, "The ship's Regimental Sergeant Major can go anywhere on the ship."

I spoke to the soldier concerned in a very authorative and powerful voice, imitating the accent of a high ranking and important officer. I ordered him to report to the ship's R.S.M immediately and tell him of the incident. Two or three minutes later the R.S.M. appeared, how fine he looked, quite dashing, over six feet in height with a spotless uniform, and highly polished Sam brown belt. He looked at no one, opened the door and walked in; he returned with the life belt and thrust it into the hands of the soldier concerned, with words that are unprintable. The naval officer disappeared; the RSM looked at me, first quite puzzled, then his whole face lit up with a big grin, then astonishingly he gave me a huge wink and departed; so I was on my own standing there feeling the sway of the ship as it ploughed its way through the waves. My memory of a man's utterance of just a few words had made all the difference to a difficult situation; after all, I was only a private soldier. Suddenly my thoughts were disturbed when I realized the R.S.M. was standing before me. He reappeared with clipboard and a piece of paper on it.

"Sign," he said, "This is to say you will shut all the portholes you can see here should the ship be torpedoed." "Yes Sir," I said, and signed. I had no idea how to shut a porthole but in front of me was a staircase which led to the top deck. I knew that this ship had three sister ships – one was the Duchess of Atholl which when torpedoed had sunk in four minutes. I looked at the staircase and thought long and hard as to what I should do should disaster strike. It did not! Our convoy hugged the North African coast how desolate it looked. Suddenly there was a U-Boat scare and depth charges were thrown overboard. The explosions caused the ship to shake and shudder violently. Shortly after this incident we arrived at the ancient port of Alexandria.

Disembarkation of the various troops began; the Royal Ordinance Core Contingent was the last off the ship. Standing on the deck I saw an enormous heap of coal, as big as the pit banks that I had seen at home. The coal was being moved slowly in baskets, to my amazement carried on the heads of women; women labourers no men. Their dresses were long and various bright colours. We were put on a train to be taken through the desert. We knew not to where. At a moderate speed we journeyed on. After some hours, the train came to a halt; we knew it was by a village because of the appalling smell. We crowded together to look through the carriage windows. What we saw surprised us: on the bank of sand by the track were about thirty or so young girls, half naked, they were waving to us. They seemed full of joy, they were all sitting together then suddenly one of their number stood up; I shall never forget what I saw. Her skin was white; her face looked pale in contrast to those around her and her lovely flaxen hair floated in the wind.

We all knew she would never know her father. I looked at the young soldiers in the carriage; cheeks reddened with the unaccustomed sun had tears rolling down them. Decades later I was to hear a lecture at Oxford; at the end of his lecture, the lecturer said with a catch in his voice, "Always remember, that the cost of sin is always borne by the innocent." All eyes were fixed on the lecturer, but not mine; I put my head in my hands and felt it difficult to hold back the tears. I thought of the white girl with her beautiful hair blowing in the Egyptian wind.

So we arrived in the dead of night at Tel-Al-Kabier. Although very late at night we were taken to have a meal. The amount of food placed in front of us was amazing. We could help ourselves to whatever and how much we wished. Accommodation was in bell tents, no beds, no blankets; we slept on the desert sand with a ground sheet.

The next day I was taken ill with dysentery. I was taken by ambulance to a military hospital half an hour by road. The doctor who attended to me was an Italian prisoner of war, and spoke perfect English. After two weeks I was considered well enough to return to my unit by army truck. I was met by a Sergeant Major who said my unit had departed. Two other men who like me had been left behind. One was a

Corporal. The S.M said we were to go to a destination in Iraq. He gave papers to the Corporal, which indicated the route we were to take. The journey would be mainly by train and after a meal we would start that evening. We boarded a train with carriages no better than cattle trucks with crude seats. As night came, we crept under the seats to sleep. We reached Haifa where there were two sets of railway lines, one from Egypt and one that went to Damascus. The Damascus line was narrow gauge. We were told New Zealanders built it in the First World War. It passed its way through the barren hills, eventually reaching the outskirts of Damascus. A heavy rainstorm occurred and as we were dressed in khaki uniforms, we became soaked. When we reached the British army camp, our accommodation was a tin hut with a concrete floor. No beds, no blankets, the food was very primitive. Early in the morning an R.S.M. appeared to tell us to be ready for rifle inspection. We were accordingly lined up, I at the end of the line. He grumbled harshly at everyone then came to me. I purposely gave him a look intended to kill. I knew my mother and her mother had done this with powerful results. It had the desired effect he simply walked past me. We were then taken to a transit camp on the outskirts of Baghdad. Next day we were taken by truck to the railway station that would take us to Basra. This was a single-track railway line and we travelled at approximately 25 M.P.H. As we waited there for transport I looked at my rifle and it was black with flies. I realised then, my hands were the same. Soon, to our relief, the truck arrived and we were taken to the base ordinance depot that seemed to be one of many building that were scattered; this is called dispersal, in case of aerial bombardment. We were taken to three or four large buildings made of corrugated iron. On the roof was heaped three or four feet of sand, no windows. Inside were some thirty beds made of sailcloth and rough timber. I found an empty bed and claimed it. Nearby was a cookhouse and some distance away was a latrine, which was a fifteen-foot trench. In the morning we were taken approximately two miles by truck to our place of work. This consisted of a large building that was made of mud-bricks in which we were to perform our allotted tasks. In my case it was checking vouchers by which units in the district applied for stores. In some cases this was difficult as some stores were of American origin. We had few actual military duties, however on one occasion I remember mounting guard over a Russian soldier who was going to be sent back to Russia.

Though only a Private, I was made for one night only a Duty Officer. About two am, two Indian Officers appeared they looked wondrously happy and told me they had shot dead a Persian who was trying to get through the perimeter fence. I praised them and made the appropriate entry. I knew that sometimes thieves would put boots on a little girl and send her through the minefield to mark the ground for places to tread with safety. I knew I was in a place where human wickedness knew no bounds. I thanked God that they had not reported an incident of that nature.

Then unexpectedly, a few days later; the officer in charge, a Major, sent for me and told me the next day to have my small kit bag ready to go with another soldier to a signals station twenty to thirty miles away to be trained as a Tele-printer Operator. We were taken by truck across miles of desert to where the signal station was. A Company Sergeant Major met us, whose words of greeting I will always remember. He said, "You must remember there are many suicides here, because men find it difficult to learn the Morse Code." He also told us that we would not see the Colonel as he was being treated for syphilis. Then we were led to our quarters where the bed consisted of three pieces of wood across two planks. No blankets; that was all we had to sleep on. Still better than the floor, which was concrete. There were few occupants of the station but all highly skilled. The small dining room was next to an open sewer. It was terrible; the smell was so bad I found it difficult to eat. We were allowed two weeks to learn to be efficient operators as the messages we received and sent were of great importance. On completing the course we returned to our unit. When I arrived I was not taken to the place I had left; I was told I had been transferred to Company Headquarters, which meant a different camp in a different place. The barracks consisted of several small compartments with three to a room. On my bed was my equipment already waiting for me. The next day I was taken to my new place of work, being driven by a Warrant Officer. I now found myself part of the Chief Ordinance Officer's Staff. With this came a certain amount of privilege. Then came the summer months. We were only allowed to work a short time in the very early morning, afterwards we were instructed to lie on our beds until the cool of the evening, which was meal time. As we lay on our beds some men made jokes, some told humorous tales about themselves; one man said he went on his honeymoon on a tandem from somewhere in Yorkshire to Blackpool and when he got there he found that one of the brakes was jammed full on. He boasted that the story with his name was printed in the local paper. He also told us that he kept a grass snake in his pocket as a pet.

The author with two companions returning home.

The man on the right of the picture is the man who had the snake. The man in the middle was a town counsellor for Manchester, and was a member of the third order of Saint Francis; he obtained entry into a Roman Catholic monastery for us. I am on the left.

He told us of the occasion when he entered the

enormous office where there were two to three hundred ATS girls employed; he took it out of his pocket and put it on a desktop. The result was immediate: the office was emptied at a record speed. I think his Commanding Officer decided he would be better employed somewhere else. So he ended up in Iraq where he kept a small lizard and spent some time catching flies with which to feed it. The last I saw of him was at Calais where I put my kitbag in the train window where I could see it, and make it easy to find my place.

However, look as I might, I could not find it. Eventually I did; he told me he had put it on the floor to help me. His name is long forgotten now. At this time I shared a room with Sandy Wilson who became famous as the author of the "Boy Friend". He had Gibbons' Decline and Fall of the Roman Empire flown out to him. This he let me read during the hot season. I knew that Churchill had read it during the hot season in India. The "English" in it is wonderful and reading it avidly affects one's own ability to write and speak English.

Sandy Wilson and his friends formed a poetry group. I was not invited, but listened to their efforts. I formed the opinion that their reading of poetry had as much meaning as it would have had, had it emitted from a dead parrot. I thought of my friend Joe Higgins while a pupil at Handsworth Grammar School; he had been ordered out of a chemistry class by an irate teacher who had supposedly became fed up with his lack of ability. While waiting in the passageway out side the class room Joe composed a short poem. This was printed in an amateur poetry magazine. It had no title but I will give it one, I called it:

Gibbet Hill

(which is the name of a road between Kenilworth and Coventry, where there was in olden times, I have been informed, a Gibbet)

I have heard the village gaffers tell
of Tom the keeper's lad.
Who beat upon the road to hell
and drove his Mother mad.

And when the cold has warped the moon
And frostily the chill winds moan,
It's Tom upon the Gallows tree,
Who shrivels, and twists, and groans.

Having thought of Joe Higgins' poem I thought I would try one myself.

Fire over London

When the walls of Empire tremble
at the shock of awful strife
and the men of mighty nations fought with
frantic strength for life.
Then they manned the flaming rampart and
seized the searing sword with scorn
and from out the great inferno this, their
finest hour, was born.

When I became the unit's tele-printer operator I shared an office with the chief ordinance officer's staff, mostly men doing correspondence. The men in the office were in charge of a chief clerk who exerted considerable influence he spent most of his time telling others what to do. He would go in and out of the chief ordinance office. Then suddenly it was announced the chief ordinance officer was to be replaced. It was at this time I received a message over the tele-printer that the war in Europe was over. The well-being of all at the depot depended on the sort of person the chief ordinance officer was. In his particular case, I never saw him. His replacement came as a Colonel Snook, who proved to be an excellent man for the job. At the same time a Staff Sergeant White, who was always referred to as "Chalky White", replaced the chief clerk.

Then we received a blow: it had been decided by the War Office in London that Colonel Snook should be seconded to the Iraqi Army. In due course his replacement arrived, who was very much disliked by everyone. He would not allow any mistakes to be made. All concerned had to endure this state of affairs. He appointed a major in charge of our office, making Chalky White's position very difficult. In the camp life went quietly on. Came the time when I was unexpectedly ordered with a few others to go on recuperation leave to Beirut. This meant travelling some hundreds of miles across the desert to the edge of the Mediterranean Sea. It was then that we all learnt that Japan had surrendered. It was a time of great joy and thankfulness. On return, I came back via Baghdad. A desert had to be crossed first. During that time I thought I would walk into the desert on my own. I reached a point when nothing was visible except sand and the sky above. I can only say to be alone in those circumstances, one is totally conscious of the presence of God. I remember the scriptures of "John the Baptist" and our Lord. The desert can be a frightening place. Indeed, the experience was one that I will never forget. I arrived at Baghdad and saw it for the last time. Then by train to Basra and the ordinance depot, after being back for some weeks. I received a tele-printer message that Baghdad would be out of bounds to British troops in a few weeks. A Colonel from Baghdad replaced the Colonel in charge of our depot as the Baghdad ordinance directorate was to be closed. Demobilisation would slowly begin to take place. Everyone was waiting for his or her demobilisation papers to arrive.

At Basra there was a market where local silversmiths sold their wares. Endless men sold watches of all sorts and types. I did not buy any watches, but bought silverware; a fine set of napkin rings I purchased to bring home as a present for my mother. I also bought bangles for my sisters. Just after I received the date of my return to England, I with some other fellows went one evening to Basra. We were astonished at the lights and were amazed to see flying boats sailing through the air, the portholes aglow with light. The whole picture seemed ethereal and unreal. As we walked through the well lit streets we came upon an Indian music hall all lit up; a show was in progress. The front door opened and an Indian gentleman stepped forward to invite us in to see the show. The quality of the performance was far beyond our expectations and we formed a high opinion of what Indian people could do. In due course we caught a truck which took us back to the depot. Since we were nearing our time for departure, we were excused all duties. One could now dream of going home. The long wait seemed to never end until our demobilisation papers were received; we were given numbers and we had to wait until our number was received.

So I come to the journey back home.

To cross the desert the army provided civilian transport, which consisted of two or three coaches. During this journey a most fearful thunder and lightning storm occured, however,we reached Damascus. The army facilities were much improved since my previous visit. We then boarded trucks, destination unknown; two Colonels using their rank re-routed the convoy in such a manner as it would pass through the Holy Land. They said this was for the benefit of the soldiers who would never get such a chance again. I felt I was fortunate indeed, as I saw Cana where Jesus performed his first miracle at a wedding ceremony. We passed through Nazareth where

I was amazed to find it was much modernised; at least I felt so. The first thing to see was Lake Galilee: it was blue and beautiful. I remembered Lord Bryon's poem,

The Destruction of Sennacherib

The Assyrian came down like the wolf on the
fold.
And his cohorts were gleaming in purple and
gold;
And the sheen on his spears was like stars on
the sea,
When the blue wave rolls nightly on deep
Galilee.

Eventually we arrived at Haifa and then boarded a train to take us to Egypt. The train was crowded with soldiers and I was forced to ride standing on the buffers between two carriages for four and a half hours. Eventually we arrived at Alexandria. We then learned that we had travelled on the incorrect train, and not on the one that had been provided.

German prisoners of war guarded the barracks, armed with pick-helves, as much of the populous were not to be trusted because of their attitude to us. After a few days we were taken to the quay where a ship waited to take us across the Mediterranean. This ship had been used in Canada as a ferryboat, and it was flat bottomed; a violent storm blew up and we were relieved when land was in sight. We landed at Toulon; to disembark we had to pick our way over the hulks of French submarines, which had remained half sunk in the harbour to prevent use of them by the Germans. We then boarded a train to Calais, a 36-hour journey from Toulon. When we arrived at our destination we entered a small camp to await transport across the channel. As we walked out, we suddenly realised that we were facing the Duke of Windsor; about eight of us stood round him and he chatted to us. Some men ran to get cameras. The Tannoy told us to treat him with respect. The advice was not necessary; a group of French girls from the kitchens just stared at him. They ate him with their eyes. We then boarded the ship to cross the channel. I heard a thick Scots accent behind me and there stood the same man from Glasgow who had been behind me when I joined the army six years before!

We were taken to an army demobilisation centre. The army then gave us our new civilian clothes, money and a ticket to our nearest railway station. In my case it was Stratford-on-Avon. At Stratford-on-Avon I walked to the townsquare and found a lone taxi. I arrived home about midnight. I had been six years in the army. I thanked God and still do. To me I had done the impossible. So ended the unforgettable.

Chapter 5

After so long away I was at last home. I woke up in the morning feeling it was my first day of freedom. I was in England. I could hear the sounds of the birds and the wind as it shook the trees. I was now in civil life; I was blessed indeed, so much to thank God for. Yet life would be different. Since my birth I had lived in a town; now I was to live in the countryside. No streets and houses but lanes and fields. No factories but simply fields of crops. So where would I find work? I visited the local labour exchange and was told they only had vacancies for farm workers or servants such as chauffeurs. I decided it would take a certain amount of time to settle down to my new situation. My circumstances were new to me; I was living in a small village, one amongst many other small villages. These villages were rarely a few miles apart; each village had its own parish church and in those days every two parishes had its own incumbent, with a residence being a vicarage or rectory. Landed gentry usually occupied the largest house or hall in the village. Some were landowners and this ownership was sometimes extensive. I knew of one family that owned thirty three thousand acres of land in the Cotswolds, which consisted of several farms. Thus the power of certain individuals was very great indeed. I felt there was enormous class divide. The whole social climate was completely different from that which I had been used to. I had to accept that I was living in a new world. One's feelings and outlook had to be adjusted to the new circumstances. Sometimes I found the very rich could be kind and benevolent. I sometimes thought how different my life had been in Handsworth Birmingham, where I had friends and acquaintances. In this new situation I only found such among elderly bell ringers with whom I could spend some happy moments. I did eventually get a job working for the Post Office at Shipton-on-Stour. I went for a short course at the main post office at Stratford-on-Avon and was then given the job of being in charge of the sorting office. This also meant I was responsible for much else as well. My many duties were too many to state here. I had to work under the sub-postmaster, a Mr. Hancock. Mr. Hancock I found to be of high intelligence whose instruction helped me to be successful at my work. Suffice it to say I had to open the door at five thirty in the morning and finished at seven in the evening. Six days a week and two hours on Sunday; all this for the princely sum of four pounds a week. This was 1947, the winter of very deep snow. We had to contend with the vehicles stuck in snow, impassable roads and the like. We did our jobs so well that we received a commendation, I think from London. We were under the Postmaster at Stratford-on-Avon; this man sent a letter to our Postmaster to say he had found a postman driver sitting on a mailbag on his driving seat: "It was the misuse of a mailbag." The next day our Postmaster went with our postman driver to Stratford; he then wrote to the Stratford Postmaster and told him he had found sixteen bags in his office all being misused.

I left and obtained a position as a costing clerk in a concrete factory.

This was a newly built factory. It was while I worked there that I married. I first saw my wife-to-be just before I went abroad while in the Army. She was talking to her parents after playing the church organ for a church service, which I had attended. Now a civilian, I went to evensong at Honington Church where she was still organist. I asked to be introduced to her, and afterwards walked with her almost to her home. With my strong connections to the church we fell in love and married; we spent our honeymoon at Swanage. When we returned I said I had thought of being a lay reader. She said she thought I would be good at it. I had to take four quite difficult examinations but I became a lay reader and started to take services at the many village churches scattered over the Cotswolds' various churches. My wife continued to play the organ and came with me when she could. She only ceased to play when she had been pregnant for a time. The birth was beset with problems, so the matter was handled by a first rate gynaecologist; she gave birth to a beautiful baby girl by Caesarean section. We felt as one in the ensuing happiness we had together. My work as a lay reader continued. A certain amount of theological training was given to lay readers, which enabled me to be proficient in my work. This experience continued for approximately seven years, during which I gained invaluable experience. Eventually I decided to apply to be trained for the full time ministry. I was flatly turned down. My rejection was followed by correspondence from the clergyman responsible for ordination training; he wrote and told me to ignore my rejection and continue to follow the course of instruction he would give. I found his words to me gave me great encouragement. This was just as well, as I could hardly leave a wife and baby to go and be trained; in those days there were no training schemes from home. I waited two or three years, my child was now older, and I had changed my job for one that brought in more money, as I had to save for the period when I would not be at work.

Bishop Linton knew all about my efforts to enter the ministry before the war, so I wrote to him regarding my situation. He replied with a letter of encouragement. I also heard from my own diocesan bishop and I saw him at his request. I next had to apply before a board of clergy, who gave me their approval. The one man responsible for training was an archdeacon and he insisted I passed a special examination, which he would set. These examinations consisted of three long essays on theological subjects. I duly submitted these papers to him. In reply I received a letter to say that I was to attend an interview with the Principal of Ripon Hall, Oxford.

Then came the sad news that my brother Bernard, serving in the Navy, had been killed by accident. I escorted his wife to his military funeral. He left three small children and I felt it was my duty to do all I could to help them. Shortly afterwards my father retired, and so I knew that once I left work I could not expect help of any sort from my family; their own needs were much too great. Fortunately my wife's family helped in very many ways when the time came that we really did need help. The lay reader's body to which I belonged also provided much-needed financial assistance. I knew how great a burden would fall on my wife. The interview would obviously be with the intention for me to go to Oxford for my training.

Chapter 6

Ripon Hall normally only accepted students with good degrees; it was a graduate college with access for its students to attend the university. Down the years a voice sounded, "What are you doing here?" But as then, a hand was reaching out to take me in. So I travelled to Oxford to have an interview with Bishop Allen, Principal of Ripon Hall. From the start he was friendly and made me feel at ease. He asked me how many services I had taken as a lay reader; when I said last year I took thirty-eight he looked amazed. He questioned me about the books I had read. I told him I read reviews if I did not have time to read them. I told him of a long sermon I had heard on the meaning of the categorical imperative, how it contrasted with Bishop Linton's, "I come to preach Christ Crucified." Finally I mentioned I had been on a mission with Gypsy Smith, a well-known evangelist. Also, I said I would always remember I heard a brilliant sermon by the Provost of Birmingham Cathedral; long afterwards I learnt that at that time, Bishop Allan had been Archdeacon of Birmingham. He must have known the person about whom I was speaking. He told me of certain books I should read. He told me it would be over one year before I could come to the College.

As we neared the time for my departure to college, unexpectedly the clergyman responsible for training turned up at our house to see us. Just before he left he said to my wife, "If there are difficulties, remember you have a friend at court." So the day came that I left home to go to Oxford. I saw my wife and child waving me off at the top of Idlicote Hill. My daughter said, "God bless you my Daddy,"; I wept and wept all the way to the bus stop. Not for myself, but for those I had left behind me. Finally I arrived at Ripon Hall, and was allotted a room. When evening came I had to attend the evening meal. I entered the large dining room; on its walls were hung large oil paintings of previous principals of the college. There was one single table of enormous size surrounded by chairs. I entered and students sat where they wished, except for the high table where the Principal and those in high authority sat. All the faces were new to me, as indeed was the atmosphere. I felt this more so when the Grace in Latin was intoned. Many other students were new as it was a new term. Engaging in conversation, we began to know each other. Three of us were older, being forty years of age. I found that I and the other two were the only ones without a university degree. However, I was treated as an academic equal. Nevertheless I was entering academic education which was based on the University principles, which I was to discover would involve lectures, reading prescribed books, writing essays, and attending tutorials and seminars. Tutorials usually involved small groups of students, but not always so – sometimes, it was one-to-one teaching.

One tutorial I had to attend concerned the matter of singing, and many services we had to study needed knowledge of music.

As a boy at school during singing lessons I was often told to keep quiet. The headmaster would sometimes shout out, "Stop singing, that boy who is making a noise like a tin can." So it was with some trepidation I took a bus to Oxford for private tuition. I was surprised to find that the gentleman teaching me was kind and helpful. He taught me to sing in tune; the whole course lasted six weeks. It helped me to appreciate the musical side of the Church of England services.

My first day ended with the service of Compline. I was ordered to hire a gown for a few pounds a term. The morning service began early. Sometimes Holy Communion followed, but not always; certain students disagreed with this, but their protests were ignored. They would have preferred Holy Communion every morning. The principal views were that the college should be acceptable to all forms of churchmanship. Breakfast followed, often only porridge. A brief rest, then we all attended a seminar, about forty to fifty students around a large table in the spacious library. Sometimes this became the scene of some argument. I was once involved in one of these, an argument; it concerned the use of elements in the Communion Service. My protagonist, a certain Dennis Ede (who became an Archdeacon), asserted that only bread and wine should be used and nothing else in the Communion Service, saying, "It says bread and wine and that is what should be used." I replied, "There is a book called 'The Dark side of the Moon' in which it describes how a few men were taken by train to be executed. In the carriage they decided they would have their last communion but the only elements that they had were water and rice so the communion was held with these instead of bread and wine." My argument was in the context of the service; once consecrated, they fulfilled the requirements of the sacrament. I am happy to recall that the Principal in this matter advised I was correct. Dennis was most magnanimous. At Ripon Hall I found myself among good friends. Next there were lecturers until lunchtime. On one occasion we had a visiting lecturer (his name I can no longer recall), who on commencing his lecture made a disparaging remark regarding our senior student. The principal of the college stopped him immediately and said, "We have a large pond in the grounds of this establishment, into which we throw lecturers we do not like." Surprise and appreciation from the students greeted this remark.

One day we met for a seminar. I had to read a

paper concerning service notes and had to write regarding social change during a period in the 19th century. Previously at this meeting, concern had been expressed about a missing book from the library; it was a book recording Lord Shaftesbury's life story. Its disappearance was accepted as a mystery. Towards the end of my paper I referred to the work of Lord Shaftesbury. The moment I mentioned his name, the whole room erupted into hysterical laughter. The Principal looked on perplexed and I too could not understand why the students found this so amusing. It was felt afterwards that I had been the instigator of the loudest laughter heard at the college.

After lunch there were essays to write and books to read. Twice a week we went to Christ Church to listen to the Regis Professor of Divinity, a brilliant theologian, one Leonard Hudson. We were not allowed to take notes but were provided with printed copies to take away after his lecture. The second day I was there I meet Jack Milverton who was a university lecturer in psychology. He helped me in many ways; he had a high opinion of my intelligence and me, and said so. This was encouraging, as I had no scholastic qualifications. Examination papers that were completed by students had to be sent from the college to the examining chaplain, then to the bishop. These were examinations that had to be passed before one could become a deacon. Many passed these examinations. I was chosen to preach at a large London church when the whole college went to London on a mission. Towards the end of my training period, I was taken by car to preach in front of Doctor Major; previously he had been principal of Ripon Hall, and was a well-known great scholar. As I spoke he moved his hearing aid in front of the pulpit to hear me better, and after supper he gave me one of his original works; he inscribed in the front cover, from the author to the preacher; he signed and dated it. This is one of my most valued possessions to this day.

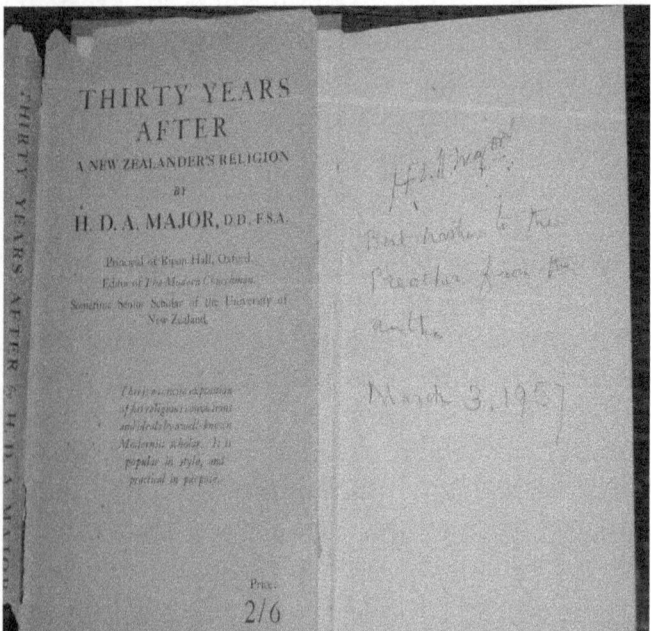

Proudly possessed by the author of this book.

Eventually, I was made a deacon. This service was performed by the then Bishop of Coventry in the parish church at Leamington Spa. My wife attended the service. I was to service my title as a curate at Saint Nicholas, Radford, Coventry. Working in a parish was part of the learning process. I was fortunate in having a good vicar.

The Rev. F.H.Oldnall - bottom left

Chapter 7

The vicar and his wife were very kind to us, but they left and I found myself in charge of a parish of 17,000 people. It was one Saturday when there were four weddings. I knew that legally a deacon could take weddings, but really it was a job reserved for the priests, and I was not yet a priest. The church wardens told me they would stand by me should I receive criticism for taking weddings. Eventually there came the Saturday. I took the three weddings; the last wedding involved a gentleman who was a freeman of the City of Coventry, with the result that the local press printed the details of the wedding in the Coventry evening paper. There was I shown as a deacon performing the ceremony. Monday morning I had a visit from the rural dean. He was furious; he just went wild at me, and of course there were no signs of the church wardens. I decided to ignore his show of bad temper. That same day I had a visit from the principal of my theological college; and when I told him of this affair, he said I was within my rights and I was to take no notice of the rural dean. Next, I was to pass the examination for the priesthood. The chief examiner was the Archdeacon of Coventry and I was congratulated on my essays. After a short time I was moved to Stratford-on-Avon. We were glad of the move as it meant taking my wife back to the countryside near her parents; where her heart was; she deserved it.

Chapter 8

Stratford-on-Avon

With Archdeacon Proctor's influence I was
sent to Stratford-on-Avon. I was to be given
charge of a daughter church; this was Saint
James the Great. When I arrived there, Canon
Prentice took me to see this church. I was
amazed at what I saw, the words are not too
much to describe as magnificent. It was built of
white stone in 1855 as a chapel of ease. It was
four years after a church of similar appearance
was built at Kenilworth, which still stands today.
Looking inside I was astonished at its size, and
how well it was appointed. Its layout contained
a side chapel. The most striking feature was a
fine east window. It even had an excellent organ
built by Harrison. It had a regular contract
ongoing for its maintenance. The chancel was
huge and contained beautifully made choir
stalls, which had correctly appointed places
for the incumbent and his curate. Beautifully
constructed arches flanked the nave. In the

building was a large wooden war memorial for the fallen of two World Wars. There was also an impressive vestry. The records of the church show it even had a church bell cast by the firm Meirs, which I happened to know was the oldest established firm in the country. Near to the west door was an impressively large font. Between the church and the road was a large well-kept lawn; unlike most churches this had a toilet approached from outside the building, which on Mop Day was securely locked.

The vicar also took me to see the Church at Bishopton, which was a small village church, but had an excellent organ, which my wife played when I took services there on Sunday afternoons. The whole church was in good repair. These two buildings would be the scene of my work; both had excellent church wardens and an excellent church life. My work at the parish church proved to be quite onerous with several services there, especially with regard to weekdays as the senior curate assisted on Sundays. My own two churches formed the basis of the people I worked with in the parish.

I must recall my gratitude for the help given to me. Taking into consideration the high educational standard of the congregation, I was forced to ensure that my sermons were prepared well and of sound order. I noticed a gentleman actor one Sunday morning taking down my sermon in short hand. I also had to take lessons at the local Church of England school where the staff occasionally complimented me on my work there. A diocesan inspector's team asked me to send a syllabus of the lessons given. I was heavily criticised, as they said there was insufficient evidence of the work of the church. I can understand this, as it was my aim to inculcate into the minds of the children the main points of the Christian religion.

My own theological education had been received at a college known for its liberal and modern views. This was reflected in what and how I taught.

As priest in charge we moved to St James House, Maidenhead Road, Stratford-on-Avon. It came as a great surprise to be told I was there on a three-month trial period. To finish my post-ordination training, I had to go to Balliol College, Oxford, to listen to a lecture by an eminent theologian. He spoke about Church unity. He was so excellent and eloquent I took copious notes of all he said. A few days after, Canon Prentice came to the house and told me that I had to give a lecture at my home to the Stratford Brotherhood, which consisted of clergy from various denominations, in and around Stratford. Some I knew to be of high scholastic attainment. I felt God had prepared the way as I had my notes on the very subject. The largest room in the house was filled; my wife was the perfect hostess. After the lecture Canon Prentice whispered to me, "You can forget the three-month trial period." The Church of Saint James the Great went from strength to strength. The congregation continued to increase.

At Holy Trinity Church on Sheakespeare's birthday a special civic service was held, during which ambassadors from various countries brought wreaths to be laid in the sanctuary on Shakespeare's tomb; I with two other curates had the job of attending to this. One felt in the presence of illustrious company when one took a wreath from men representing the most powerful nations. As I looked down the body of the church towards the great west door that I had never seen opened, I was always impressed by the large Victorian stained glass window over its top. Some said it lacked subtlety. I felt, as did others, that it was intensely powerful with its myriad of striking colours. They were so intense they were awe-inspiring. The nave was filled with people from all parts of the world. As I looked upon the scene I was struck by how much the pillars leaned outwards, as they had done for centuries.

Our time at Stratford was a very happy time. It was at Stratford that my wife found good and faithful friends. She joined a ladies' art group, and a sewing group. My little daughter on one occasion presented the famous actress Dame Edith Evans with a bouquet. I should mention when I preached at the Guild Chapel it was Ascension Day and the Head Master of Stratford-on-Avon Grammar School took the service for the boys there. I shall never forget the scene in the church as the boys sat in rows in their smart uniforms. They were privileged to attend the same school that Shakespeare had attended. When I stood to speak the atmosphere seemed bathed in history. I spoke of the command of our Lord to preach the

Gospel throughout the world. Usually Canon Prentice would have preached but this time he sent me instead. In the vestry afterwards the Head Master congratulated me on my sermon. I felt I had upheld the trust that Canon Prentice had placed upon me. The time came for us to leave Stratford; so what memories would I take with me? One stood out and it was not anything I did. I was just there the moment it took place. I was asked to visit a Mrs. Wilson whose husband had passed away. This man had been a most important figure. He had occupied a high position at the Treasury when, during the war, it had been moved from London to Stratford-on-Avon. Taking into account the deceased was so well known in high places, a very large congregation was expected. The atmosphere was such as I had never known before. Canon Prentice had ordered me to attend the funeral service but not to take part in the proceedings. At the appropriate time the coffin was lifted shoulder high; it was then that from one high clerestory window came a sudden beam of most powerful sunlight which rested on the coffin, then suddenly from all the clerestory windows came down immense shafts of brilliant streams of bright, strong light. A picture was presented of beams of light that seemed as solid as any sculptured masonry. Slowly the cortège moved forwards towards the end of the church. For the first time I saw the great west door slowly opened; the service was ended. The last journey was about to begin. In the intense sunlight a silent voice within me knew God had spoken, it was very real. In the sacred moment, almighty God was with us. In the church the congregation did not seem to wish to leave, many remained in prayer. I had taken no part in the funeral service yet came away with such a memory.

John Betjeman had once told Canon Prentice that he was the finest preacher in England. However, he was now growing older and his powers were not as they once were. It was time for him to retire; when this happened my wife and I felt a great sense of loss. He was, I felt, the last of the Victorians. This was a man of great presence; and very gifted as an orator. I was fortunate to have been trained under his leadership. In due course he retired and the matter of his replacement had to be considered. The rumour was a few clergy had been asked to replace him; all had refused. I could never understand why a successor had not been looked for outside the diocese, as the church concerned was of national importance. Eventually a clergyman who was a vicar near to Coventry accepted the living. I attended the service of his induction that was conducted by the Bishop of Coventry. I remember the new incumbent addressing the large congregation and telling them he had come to put Stratford-on-Avon on the map. This boastful remark boded doubtful success in his incumbency. Within a few weeks of his becoming incumbent he resigned. I do not remember who his successor was. At the time I had accepted a living in the diocese of Derby so it was time for pastures new.

Chapter 9

Rosliston

The Principal of my theological college, Bishop Allen was made Bishop of Derby; and as such he invited me to accept a living and be vicar in his diocese. I was sent to see the Patron of the living who was a Mr. Neilson of Caton Hall, Derbyshire. Mr. Neilson was a New Zealander and had inherited a country mansion and the large estate from his deceased uncle. I noticed a complete absence of servants when he and his wife invited both my wife and myself. He told me the bishop had asked him what type of man he would prefer. He had told the bishop that these places needed a missionary. These words were truly prophetic. So I became the Vicar of Rosliston and Coton-in-the-Elms, in the Diocese of Derbyshire. I found that there was a great contrast to what I had left at Stratford. I had left an excellent modern house. The large Victorian vicarage that we were to now reside in was in a bad state of repair and had been so for a number of years. I informed the archdeacon; he showed no sympathy, but told me it had once been far worse. He also told me we were fortunate to have running water connected; previous incumbents had to rely on drawing water from a well in the garden. In recent years it had a flushing toilet installed; most houses in the village did not have this luxury. Neither did the two schools. This was of great concern to me; I was chairman of the board of Governors and I felt this state of affairs was disgraceful. The local council eventually took up the whole matter. Later, I learnt that another vicar's wife had visited the house and when she entered the front door, refused to go further. The bishop's wife paid us a visit and was quite upset at what she saw. Some small improvements were made and a cooking stove installed in the kitchen. There was no central heating. An old copper was found in the adjoining scullery. A door in the far corner led to the cellar, which in winter flooded. We had the occasional frog and toad that would make an appearance much to my wife's discomfiture.

In the kitchen fixed to a wooden board just below the ceiling were a line of bells; below each bell was the corresponding room the bell was located in. To summon a maid to a specified room a lever was pushed; there were two levers to each room, each located either side of the fire grate. These were relics from earlier days. A very elderly lady in the parish had been a kitchen maid in her early years and she recounted tales of the past days to my wife and daughter.

My daughter found in the attic a decrepit bath chair and bed-rest which in former years was kept in many vicarages for use, when required by the villagers. We, including my growing daughter, had to simply endure it. We invited several members of the Church council to attend a meeting at the vicarage; none came. I was told no one could speak freely in someone else's house. Further meetings in both parishes were held in buildings allied to the church. Well, that meant we did not have to provide refreshments. Important changes were afoot; the first basic change was the building of a sewer in both villages. Further changes followed with the building of new roads, followed by a new housing development. This latter event was to have a profound effect upon the character of the villages. The new families brought in workers of a different type. No longer was the village predominantly populated by farm workers, but by men of important trades. A huge power plant at nearby Drakelow provided new types of employment.

I was astonished to be told while taking down information regarding a parishioner that his job was that of a turbine driver. Changes were taking place all around, even the great breweries at Burton-on-Trent were being modernised.

Occasionally we had visitors from my first curacy at Coventry. It seemed changes were taking place further afield. My wife and I received news that unfortunately proved to be a shock; we were told that the Church Saint James the Great at Stratford-on-Avon had been demolished. It was difficult to make enquiries about this but I did learn that the beautiful east window had been reinstated in another church on the south coast. Reports reached me that the congregation were saddened and found it difficult to find another place of worship. I could only share with them their sadness.

After a few weeks I decided I would print our own monthly church magazine and give it free to every house in both parishes. I purchased a duplicating machine, paper and ink. The difficulty lay in doing the stencils. All this took quite a time, and then printing was an all day job. Volunteers took the papers round the houses.

One man aggressively told me the lady that had delivered his magazine had only lived in the parish two years. However, after a few months it was quite a success. People began to look forward to receiving it. To me it was an attempt to evangelise and get a message across, and slowly but surely people responded.

Then an unpleasant occurrence took place; walking into Rosliston church I found a large part of the ceiling had collapsed. I sent for the diocesan architect who said, "Perhaps it would be better if the church were demolished." I expressed my strong disagreement, and under his direction the church ceiling was repaired.

I had good support from Rosliston's village school's Head Master, Mr. Baker, whose scholarship was such that I could not understand why he was teaching at such a small school. I learnt later that he was an exemplary scholar of

Latin.

He had devoted 36 years to the people of Rosliston. He had helped many a family to compose letters, or had given wise advice when asked. As he grew older, he became frailer; his health gradually declined and he retired to his bed. He died peacefully and was blessed; his funeral was a most sad occasion, it seemed that the whole village wept. I told the congregation that there would never be a long serving schoolmaster again. Time proved my words to be true.

A lady of the parish came to see me in great distress. Her son-in-law had been summoned to court; he had been apprehended by the police after causing damage to motor vehicles whilst in a drunken state. It was Christmas time and he had been delivering coal. Several house occupants had given him alcoholic drink in the Christmas spirit. In a drunken state he had done considerable damage. I gave the lady a name of a solicitor who would defend him in court and I promised to be there to speak in his favour. When asked by the magistrate to do so, I looked across the court and saw him, bent, with his head in his hands; he looked a sorry figure. In my early youth I had read Alexander Dumas's "The Count of Monte Cristo"; I remembered a court scene in the book when a gentleman addressing the magistrate simply said, "Just look at him." In the book I remembered the dramatic effect of these words. So I began with the words, "Just look at him." To the relief of many he was only fined and not imprisoned. I rarely appeared at court. I was pleased that the affair had a happy ending.

With the increased population of both parishes, finances improved. The repair to the Rosliston Church ceiling proved to be the beginnings of a process of repair and improvements. Similarly at Coton-in-the-Elms the church yard was increased in size and the church maintained in good repair. Change continued even at diocesan level.

Perhaps God had moved me from Stratford because he and he alone could see a most unexpected future. I was well removed from a scene of great sadness. Then there was a sudden change: Bishop Allen came to the end of his term in office of about ten years and he decided to retire. I attended his farewell gathering with the rural dean. His wife explained they would live in a small house near Oxford. In his departing speech he remarked that he had, during his time as bishop, been forced to live in four different residences. Just before his departure I received a personal letter of appreciation. He expressed reassurance concerning his replacement. His replacement proved to be completely different and I had reason to believe he was well chosen for the task in hand. He visited our vicarage shortly after being made bishop, he looked at me and said, "Have the dilapidations board seen this?" It seemed to appear that he did not approve of the condition of the house we were living in. He referred to the archdeacon in public as "Black Jack"; Black Jack soon retired. The bishop had a genuine concern for his clergy

– even one's pay began to increase. He had connections with the Tavistock Institute in London and we had lectures about understanding human behaviour. We had to attend courses on sensitivity and people's feelings. I always addressed the rural dean as "Mr." But the next time I saw him he said, "Call me Philip"; what a change. Then one day the phone rang and the archdeacon told me the bishop wanted to take over Linton, this was a village just outside of my two parishes with a population of twelve thousand people. I took on this extra work but after a while it was decided to make this extra area of responsibility into a parish. A new vicar was found and I reverted back to my two parishes.

In the post one day I received a communication from the coal board in regard to a very modern colliery quite near the parishes. They asked for permission to extract coal from under the churchyard. I consulted the church's legal department at Derby and was told I was not to agree and also not to disagree. This advice seemed strange to me but within a comparatively short time the colliery closed.

I was appalled to find Coton-in-the-Elms school was in an awful state of decay; rats were found in the building, but it seemed impossible to persuade the local authority that a new school was urgently needed. The former Head Teacher had retired and a young lady Head Teacher, young in years and in spirit was appointed. I was still concerned about the school building. Mr. Nielson proved to be a very great help. He entered public life and became a magistrate and earned a reputation for fairness. Getting a new school proved to be a difficult business. I was told there was no hope. All seemed lost and the task hopeless, However, I saw some important people privately and put forward Coton's case. One of those important people was Mr. Neilson, he was the one I looked to for help and instead of failure success was attained. Coton's new school was authorised; yet in all this I did very little. To have the ear of just one person who sits with those in high places can determine so much in the battles of life. When it neared completion I attended a meeting and said I thought the Bishop of Derby should formally open it, as it was a church school. "No, No," I was told, we must have a political figure. The day came for the school to begin its work; the children and staff all entered the new building. Then I arrived dressed for the occasion and took the correct service of dedication, and formally opened the school.

I then requested the Head Teacher, Mrs. Lakin, to make the first entry in the new school diary, which was to record what had been done. I suppose that entry still exists.

Then a few people at Coton formed a small choir. On two occasions they sang the Crucifixion. They also sang at Christmas time together with Beryl Coates; Mrs. Lakin also brought in the school children. These were for all of us very happy times.

A humorous occasion occurred during my time at Coton-in-the-Elms; an elderly lady stood over her husband's grave and threw a bucket of water over it and was heard to say, "That will cool you down." On the gravestone was written, "May he find in heaven the peace he never knew on earth."

Chapter 10

The taking of weddings is all part of a vicar's job. They, however, vary much in the sort of occasion they prove to be. They may be with only a small number of people present, just enough to fulfil the legal requirements. Or alternatively, one could have a full church with perhaps men in morning dress with top hats and a waiting number of limousines with chauffeurs and bedecked with ribbons. It happened just once at Rosliston, that a wedding somewhat like the latter example took place. This was towards the end of my ministry. I took the service in a packed church, all went well but in the vestry the registers had to be signed, the bride's father signed with a straight line as his signature. I protested but he said he always signed that way. So there was nothing I could do. The reception was held in the most prestigious hotel for miles around, of course we were invited. I drove my wife and I suddenly realised I was wearing my second best suit. When we entered the huge dining room, place names on the tables denoted where we were to be seated. The lady seated next to me advised me she was only there by her agent's permission. A member of the staff asked her for her autograph. She was to sing the lead part in an opera called Electra; my mind went back to the time I was fifteen years old; Olive Rose had told me how she had been taught to pronounce correctly the word electricity. The first course was shellfish and as the meal progressed she became very talkative. She seemed full of life. She had her own philosophy of life, she spoke with the assurance of an Oxford Don, and explained how people became that which they really wished to be. It was very much a matter of self-perception and the realisation of personal potential. As the meal came to its end she heard someone say the word sex, and she said jokingly, "Those are what people in Scotland carry their coal in." The next day I felt ill and developed a rash with pimples. I realised that I was allergic to shellfish. The day after I received shocking news. The same lady I had sat at table with did not arrive at breakfast at her hotel. When the police entered her room they found her sitting in a chair with the score of Electra on her lap and she was quite dead. This was not only a shock but also a mystery – it all belongs to those things in life, which we fail to understand. I must add a further few words, for she was someone possessed with a powerful spirit. Her whole being was alive with it. It seemed to me that although her unexpected death had taken her body, her essential self must live on and go wherever her God would take her. We ordinary mortals can only pray that God in his goodness will eventually allow us to follow.

Repton

Stephen Verney had earned enormous respect due to his service in World War II. Afterwards he became a well-known theologian. This man was appointed Canon Missioner in the Diocese of Coventry. I met him at a conference at Balliol College, Oxford, where I spoke at a debate. What I spoke about I have long since forgotten. However afterwards I had a visit from him so we established a friendship. When I moved to Derbyshire I was in the Deanery of Repton. Then it was decided that there should be a Bishop of Repton, and occasionally we met. (There had been a Bishop of Repton in Saxon times, he preceded the Bishop of Lichfield), and occasionally we meet. Stapenhill in Derbyshire has a very large church and was on one occasion was chosen for a very large confirmation service. I and other clergy attended but the Bishop of Repton conducted the service to a large congregation. At the end of the service the bishop led the way down the aisle; as he came to the end and was about to turn towards the west door, suddenly he was confronted by a very small boy. The boy simply stood upright and kept perfectly still. Everyone stood motionless, the organ ceased. Then the bishop slowly in front of the fair-haired little boy, leaning with his hand on his staff, went down on one knee. They just looked into each other's eyes. Everyone, everywhere was silent. The look in the boy's eyes was one of complete innocence. The innocence; that long forgotten virtue that can only be found in little children. It was a scene portraying humility. He looked into the child's wide blue eyes with a gaze beyond description. This book is about pictures from life, but was there ever a picture like this?

A prince of the church kneeling at the foot of a small child with a look in his eyes beyond description. I wished I had a camera to record the moment, but it would not have done justice to this event. No! It needed a great oil painting such as a Rubens, to capture such an immense sensitivity and catch the deep spiritual message of the moment. All who looked on would take away an unforgettable experience. I felt my life had been enriched by what I had seen.

Almost from the first day we had lived at Rosliston, we had befriended an elderly farmer named Harry Peach. He lived across the road from the vicarage. He was full of knowledge regarding the village. He became a great friend to us all; my daughter loved him. After Sunday lunch when the washing up was being done by both of them, many a cup was broken and no one said a word. Subsequently when he passed away at ninety-four years, he joined his wife in the churchyard.

An amusing incident occurred during my time as vicar of Rosliston. I was the proud owner of a Hillman Super-Minx. Eventually I sold this when I bought another car. I sold it cheaply and intended to put an advertisement in the local paper. It seemed that two men from Ireland were working for the local paper at the time. Instead of an advertisement being inserted in the paper, the two young men instead bought the car from me. In the boot of the car was a leak through which mud and water entered with some force. I stuffed the gaping hole with some fertiliser bags. The car was taken by ship to Ireland when unloaded at the port; as it was the time of political unrest an army captain ordered the car to be searched. On finding the fertiliser bags, (known to be connected with explosives), the two men were threatened with arrest. They replied, when questioned, that they had bought the car from a vicar in England. The interrogator had, I was informed, replied, "Oh yes, my Granddad is the Archbishop of Canterbury." To prove their case they produced the logbook signed by myself. They thought that the story was so good they contacted the local paper that they had worked for at Burton-on-Trent. A twisted story arose by some people in the village saying the vicar was a member of the IRA. This only served to cause me great amusement.

Among the new houses built in Rosliston was one that was especially large in size. A parishioner told me that a lady who had come to live there was extremely ill. She was a well-known educationalist and highly respected – her husband was also. He was a member of a local family, also well-known. As vicar, it was my duty to visit this lady. At my first visit I blessed her and said I would call again. A few days later I made another visit. Her condition had deteriorated; she told me sadly she had said good-bye to her children. I held her hand and prayed, suddenly she opened her eyes and whispered to me I shall call you the Rev Fred. I blessed her and time stood still. The funeral was not in church but at the local crematorium. I travelled to it fully robed and waited outside until the mourners had entered. I waited until the attendant opened the large glass doors and a pathway was made for me to reach the desk where I was to take the service. The building was crammed tight with people; to me it was a rare sight.

When the service had ended I was thanked. The atmosphere on this occasion was such that its intense sadness was reflected in my voice, I felt sensitive to the occasion. I did not take another service in that place again.

We were getting older and felt it was time for me to retire. So at the age of sixty-eight years, I retired. We lived in a bungalow in a temporary capacity before moving to Kenilworth in Warwickshire. It was while living in this bungalow I was taken in great pain and was subsequently taken to Burton on Trent General Hospital for my gall bladder to be removed. The operation was not straight forward and instead of being hospitalised for five days, it was eleven days before I was discharged. As I lay in bed after the operation two or three nurses stood at the foot of the bed and asked how I wished to be addressed, as they had realised I was a reverend. I replied, "Please call me the Rev Fred."

We, by the grace of God, eventually purchased a house in Kenilworth. We moved there with thankful hearts. My wife Muriel was in the county of her birth and I was in the diocese of my ordination. We had come home at last. Sunday came and we went to the little Church of St Barnabas, we found ourselves amongst wonderfully Christian people. At St Barnabas I took an occasional service. I had joined the prayer book society and at times was able to use the prayer book for the service. Also I at times used the King James version of the Bible.

I wrote a few pieces for the Parish magazine. I wrote one about Saint Bridget in which I stated that she became a bishop. I found that not all agreed; I wrote also about Pope Joan, but it was never published.

We became regular attendants at all the various events. We also enjoyed other things. My wife joined an art group and I resumed bell ringing. Then we were invited to live in a clergy close. As time went on I was getting older and less physically capable. I will therefore bring my narrative to a suitable close. A lady began my tale and one will end it. I was taking a weekday communion at St Nicholas Church and preaching about St James the Great; I said how his main accuser asked for his forgiveness but with little time to speak St James had cried out, "The Lord be with you," then for both the axe fell. I said those very words have resonated down the ages. We shall use them when we pass the peace. After the service I stood at the west door to shake hands as the congregation left.

When all seemed to have left the church I saw a dear elderly lady, a Miss Smallwood, coming down the aisle helped by a lady friend. When she reached me I held out my hand she clutched it and said "Thank you, Fred." I was taken aback and said to her how nice of you to call me Fred. Her reply was resolute: "I am sure God does." Those words I will never forget.

Epilogue

It is right that I should look over the years of my life and thank God for his kindness to me.

I feel that few have had my good fortune and as part of it in my old age I have recorded certain parts from the past. There were times of great joy; there were times of great sadness also.

When only about nine years old I saw at the cinema the film "The Three Musketeers"; at the end of the picture there flashed across the screen "There is a greater adventure beyond". There lies the purpose of this life.

From the Parish Magazine of Saint Nicholas:
Taken from History
(A tale of the incredible yet true)

It has been said that in the dark ages, God and his Angels slept. The worst part of this dreadful period was the ninth century.

It was during this time that a female child was born in Germany at Mainz. In her early years she went to a monastery, to be educated, at Fulda. She went disguised as a boy as girls were not allowed to enter places of learning. As time went on she became a gifted scholar, very proficient in Latin and Greek.

When a young woman she and a monk became lovers and with her disguised as a monk, she was taken to Athens. She left there and went to Rome. It was there that she, over time, gradually rose to high office in the church until eventually she was elected Pope in 855. Taking her part as a man, she occupied the papacy for two and a half years.

As she was of English descent she was known as John Anglicus. Her death was dramatic and sad. While taking part in a procession in Rome, she suddenly collapsed in pain and died in childbirth. About this event and its aftermath stories are contradictory; however no religious procession passed that way for at least a hundred years.

Her death served to prove her sex. In her short time as Pope she showed such devotion as to leave the memory of her in the hearts of many people and the church raised no objection when she became known as Pope Joan. For some five hundred years, she was highly revered, many statues were made of her; a well known one was in the Cathedral at Sienna.

With the rise of Protestantism in the seventeenth century the church made enormous efforts to erase her name from recorded history and delete all evidence of her. All her statues were destroyed including the one at Sienna. The Church she had served so well finally said that she was only a mythical figure and had never existed. It still does. Yet today, there are historians who say there are some five hundred documents which testify to her life and great attainments. I am sure quite sure that Pope Joan was real, very real. And that she was a fine intelligent lady of firm faith and astonishing personal courage.

There is Another History, which belongs to Heaven. There, though dismissed here by some, and forgotten by the many, her noble soul lives on and will do so for all Eternity.

Rev F. H. Oldnall

From Dairymaid to Bishop
A tale of the Celtic Church

"In a quiet watered land, a land of roses," so wrote an Irish poet about his native land.

It was in this beautiful setting that the Celtic Church flourished during the early centuries of Christianity. Into this land and its church was born about 451 St Brigid, as she is now remembered; although of a noble family, from her early years she was forced to work as a dairymaid. As she became older however, she grew in holiness and in devotion to God. Full of good works, she was especially kind to the poor.

When she decided to become a nun, the occasion of her receiving the veil became a miraculous event. As the bishop, named Macaille (or Mel), put his hands on her head a great light shone about her and pointed to heaven. The saintly bishop took this as a sign from God, and instantly consecrated her a bishop. It was as such that her life and works were outstanding. She was given land and a large monastery was built for both men and women. As it was of dual purpose a male bishop joined her, one Conleth. With the passage of time this monastery became an important centre of learning.

From its base in Ireland the Celtic Church sent its missionaries far into Europe and news of Brigid and what she did spread across the continent. In her own lifetime she became a legend.

She died in 525 leaving behind a name still much venerated. The Church of St Bride in London is named after her.

There are several women bishops in the United States. Yet there was one once, she lived and ministered in Ireland, and they say she was beautiful. One finds the simple words from a Celtic prayer so appropriate, "God held her in the hollow of his hand."

The Synod of Whitby, held in 664, deliberately brought an end to the Celtic Church, and also any thought of women having any equality with men in the ministry. In our own lifetime things have changed, and we now have women priests. Thankfully, in more recent times, our first female bishop, the first successor to the humble Irish lady whom God willed to be a bishop.

Reverend Fredrick H. Oldnall.

www.ingramcontent.com/pod-product-compliance
Lightning Source LLC
Chambersburg PA
CBHW021130020426
42331CB00005B/704